Isabel Zorn · Susanne Maass · Els
Carola Schirmer · Heidi Schelhowe

Gender Designs IT

I0014613

Studien Interdisziplinäre Geschlechterforschung
Band 13

Herausgegeben vom

Zentrum für interdisziplinäre Frauen- und Geschlechterforschung der Carl von Ossietzky Universität Oldenburg (ZFG), Zentrum für feministische Studien – Frauenstudien / Gender Studies der Universität Bremen (ZFS).

Isabel Zorn · Susanne Maass
Els Rommes · Carola Schirmer
Heidi Schelhowe (Eds.)

Gender Designs IT

Construction and Deconstruction
of Information Society Technology

VS VERLAG FÜR SOZIALWISSENSCHAFTEN

Bibliografische Information Der Deutschen Nationalbibliothek
Die Deutsche Nationalbibliothek verzeichnet diese Publikation in der
Deutschen Nationalbibliografie; detaillierte bibliografische Daten sind im Internet über
<http://dnb.d-nb.de> abrufbar.

1. Auflage Februar 2007

Lektorat: Monika Mülhausen

Der VS Verlag für Sozialwissenschaften ist ein Unternehmen von Springer Science+Business Media.
www.vs-verlag.de

Umschlaggestaltung: KünkelLopka Medienentwicklung, Heidelberg
Satz: Anke Vogel
Druck und buchbinderische Verarbeitung: Krips b.v., Meppel
Gedruckt auf säurefreiem und chlorfrei gebleichtem Papier
Printed in the Netherlands

ISBN 978-3-531-14818-2

Contents

I Introduction

Susanne Maass, Els Rommes, Carola Schirmer, Isabel Zorn
Gender Research and IT Construction: Concepts for a
Challenging Partnership 9

Heike Jensen
The United Nations World Summit on the Information Society:
Empowering Women as Shapers of the Information Society? 33

II Analysis and Deconstruction

Jutta Weber, Corinna Bath
'Social' Robots & 'Emotional' Software Agents:
Gendering Processes and De-Gendering Strategies for 'Technologies
in the Making' 53

Cecile K. M. Crutzen
Ambient Intelligence, between Heaven and Hell.
A Transformative Critical Room? 65

Christina Björkman, Pirjo Elovaara, Lena Trojer
Feminist Technoscience Rearranging in the Black Box of
Information Technology 79

III Construction of Information Society Technology

Susanne Maass, Els Rommes
Uncovering the Invisible: Gender-Sensitive Analysis of
Call Center Work and Software 97

Tanja Carstensen, Gabriele Winker
E-Empowerment of Heterogeneous Feminist Networks 109

Tanja Paulitz
Implicit/Explicit Alliances between Gender and Technology in the
Construction of Virtual Networks 121

IV   Education and Empowerment for the Information Society

Ruth Meßmer, Sigrid Schmitz
Bridging Disciplines: Gender Studies and Computer Science
in an E-Learning Course.. 135

Edeltraud Hanappi-Egger
Computer Games: Playing Gender, Reflecting on Gender 149

Bettina Munk
LogoGo – An Approach to the Design of Girl-Specific
Educational Software.. 161

Susann Hartmann, Heike Wiesner, Andreas Wiesner-Steiner
Robotics and Gender: The Use of Robotics for the Empowerment
of Girls in the Classroom.. 175

About the Authors.. 189

I Introduction

Gender Research and IT Construction: Concepts for a Challenging Partnership

Susanne Maass, Els Rommes, Carola Schirmer, Isabel Zorn

> "We, the representatives of the peoples of the world, [...] declare our common desire and commitment to build a people-centred, inclusive and development-oriented Information Society, where everyone can create, access, utilize and share information and knowledge, enabling individuals, communities and peoples to achieve their full potential in promoting their sustainable development and improving their quality of life, premised on the purposes and principles of the Charter of the United Nations and respecting fully and upholding the Universal Declaration of Human Rights."

This Declaration of Principles for Information Society was made during the UN World Summit of the Information Society in Geneva 2003[1].

Current transformations towards the Information Society are affecting professional and private lives, individual and societal interactions, economic and educational directions and technological developments. Or, to put it the other way around: New technologies and in particular information and communication technologies offer a multitude of opportunities for transformations in the mentioned (and many more) fields. To emphasize this close connection the EU used the term 'Information Society Technology' (IST) in their 6th Framework and put forth the "IST Vision: anywhere anytime natural access to IST services for all"[2].

1 Information Society Technology – New Opportunities for Everyone?

Notwithstanding the ideological goals of creating an 'inclusive' Information Society for 'everyone', the chances offered by Information Society are unequally distributed, e.g. by country, class, ethnicity – and by gender, the very aspect this book will focus on. Equal opportunity is the agreed-upon goal of WSIS participants. With respect to gender, the EU set out to accomplish equal opportunity by its so-called 'gender mainstreaming' strategy. This means that political actors

---

1   WSIS Declaration of Principles http://www.itu.int/wsis/docs/geneva/official/dop.html
2   http://cordis.europa.eu/ist/activities/activities.htm

need to assess the potential consequences of any decision for women and men, including those concerning implementation strategies for Information Society Technologies.

Access to and ability to use IST are the prerequisites for participation in many of today's social, cultural, political or economic activities. Lack of opportunity as well as individual abstinence, both have the same effects: being a 'non-user' of computers or the Internet means to be excluded from large parts of society, so inequalities in access and use are highly problematic. On top of this, involvement in IST design is a highly prestigious activity. Information technology business offers positions of power and good incomes for those with the appropriate (technical) education and enough self-confidence.

With respect to sex we currently find inequalities of various kinds. On a global scale the kind and quantity of IST use still differs widely. Women's access to Internet technology is generally lower than men's, and this is true not only for the South but also for the North (except for the US): According to the SIGIS report, in January 2002 women in France, Germany, UK, Norway, Denmark and Sweden accounted for about 40-45% of all Internet users, with women in Italy and Spain just below 40% (Stewart 2002, 5). The overview also lists research results which show that women use the Internet less often than men and that the individual Internet sessions by men take longer than women's (ibid.). In 2006 the percentage of Internet users among men (65.4%) was still higher than among women (51.5%) in Germany (TNS infratest 2006). Especially among people with low educational background the gender gap is much more significant.

By far the largest gender gap can be observed in IT professions. In several European countries like Germany, UK, the Netherlands, Belgium, Italy, Denmark, Austria, Finland, Sweden and France, the numbers of women researchers in engineering and technology were below 20% of total researchers in 1999, some of them even below 10% with an EU average of 12% (Stewart 2002, 18). In all major OECD countries female graduates in computing are (often far) less than 50 % of all graduates (OECD 2006). In Germany in 2004 less than 17% of all incoming students and about 16% of the graduates in the field of computing science were women, these numbers are even lower in Denmark, the Netherlands and Belgium. Countries like the UK, Italy and France have a slightly higher percentage of around 22% female graduates amongst computing scientists, whereas Finland and Sweden have the highest percentage with over 40%.

Gender research with respect to the field of computing has been done for quite some time (for an early overview see Richelmann, Schmidt 1989). The most important starting point was the perceptible gender gap in computing as described above. Gender research was done from two perspectives: from 'outside' – social scientists studied science and technology disciplines and the people involved in them; and from 'inside' – women in science and technology reflected on discipli-nary cultures and on their own biographies. Authors from both perspectives present their work in this book.

The book is based on contributions to the International Symposium 'GIST – Gender Perspectives Increasing Diversity for Information Society Technology' that took place in Bremen, Germany, in June 2004[3] (N. et al. 2004). The symposium attracted researchers from around the world and from many disciplines, sharing the goal of applying gender research to the IT sector and of supporting women's projects with adequate technology. Gender perspectives do increase the diversity in thinking about technology, its use and its users. The authors in this book will present new starting points for criticism of technology and examples for ways to actively influence IST development.

Our aim is to show that by explicitly introducing gender perspectives into IST design we have a chance not only to bridge the digital divide but also to improve IST and its construction processes in general. Today software designed for a female audience sometimes is based on very simple stereotypes that picture girls and women in traditional roles and as disinterested, even antipathetic and unknowledgeable users of technology. We hope instead that software con-struction informed by gender studies will support the deconstruction and transformation of existing assumptions and structures as far as gender relations are concerned and will lead to software and software design processes that will empower men *and* women.

The authors' disciplinary backgrounds are diverse, ranging from computing science, math and biology to philosophy and theory of science, but also scholars with a background in sociology, psychology, international management and the arts are represented. They bring together perspectives from computing science and from gender studies and they cover epistemological, technical, educational and socio-political questions. With these topics we address a variety of readers: *computing science researchers* who work on socially oriented software engineering methods or innovative technologies with an interest in encountering new perspectives on requirements engineering and paths of innovation; *software designers* interested in constructive impulses that cause them to question their own images and assumptions about the user communities they serve; *gender researchers* with an interest in examples of how to apply gender research to the fields of IST development; *computing scientists* applying for project funds as well as *policy makers* with an interest in gender mainstreaming criteria that are relevant in technology design projects; and *teachers and trainers in technology*

---

3   see www.e-gist.net

with an interest in gender-sensitive teaching practices.

The remainder of this chapter will start by defining three gender research approaches to Information Society Technology: the liberal tradition, standpoint theory and post-structuralism. In section 3 we will describe how this fits with the traditional concepts of computing science and recent trends to further open the discipline for social considerations. In section 4, we will introduce the various parts and chapters of this book.

2   Gender Studies Approaches to Information Society Technology

Although all authors in this book relate to gender studies in some way or other, their perspectives vary as much as their disciplinary backgrounds. Indeed, gender studies itself is a multi- and interdisciplinary field of research, the commonality amongst gender studies researchers in general and specifically in this book is caused by the kind of questions asked. The critical perspective is common with attention being paid to power structures and relations (making visible who bene-fits and what is invisible and/or undervalued) on the one hand and to studying and challenging existing norms, to show where changes and transformations are possible on the other. Similarly, imagining 'the' gender (sensitive) perspective or one single methodology is inherently problematic. As many gender researchers have shown, each set of standards, categorization or instrument brings its own blindness, obscures some things at the same time as it highlights others (see Bowker, Star 2000; Maass, Rommes this volume; Björkman et al. this volume). This is especially problematic in a field of research that intends to study what is being left unstudied or invisible.

Concepts and questions used in gender analyses have shifted over time as research topics and interests changed, as theoretical and political positions shifted and as different explanations for the gender gap led to different policy and research frameworks. We will introduce three perspectives, epistemologies, or research frameworks; each employing different sets of questions and each pre-senting different sets of explanations for the relative exclusion of women from the Information Society. These perspectives have also led to different kinds of measures to narrow the gender gap, some of which have been adopted by policy makers or companies. In each chapter of this book, traces of, points of inspi-ration or references to these traditions can be found. We will present the liberal tradition, standpoint theory and post-structuralism (for similar categorizations see e.g. Wajcman 2004).

In the *liberal tradition*, which is the research framework most commonly found amongst policy-makers, women and men are regarded as being equal.

However, since women have been placed in a disadvantaged position, they need support in overcoming material and other barriers that exclude them from the Information Society. So, much policy for including women in the Information Society is based on a deficit, resource or discrimination model of inclusion, meaning that women need economic, social and knowledge support to overcome their exclusion and they need support against gender discrimination at work or while pursuing an education. Within this tradition, it is more common to write about men and women, rather than about masculinities and femininities or individual men's and women's experiences. Indeed, much statistical research can also be categorized under this tradition.

Gender researchers within this tradition have made women and their work visible in the history of the development of IST, showing that women have worked in IT professions since its conception and that there is no inherent difference between men and women that disqualifies women from being competent IST designers and users (Oost 1998; Schelhowe 1991). Others within this research framework have studied discriminatory practices. Oldenziel (1997), Cockburn (1985) and Hacker (1989), for instance, have shown how types of legislations and selection criteria at work have effectively blocked women from entering technological fields. Sutton (1991) and Rasmussen and Håpnes (1991) have shown how discriminatory practices by teachers and peers at schools and universities make it harder for girls and young women to gain the required skills and knowledge. And several studies have shown that access to computers and the Internet at home and for leisure activities is more easily available for boys and men, who have more material, cultural and social resources needed for getting access (Haddon 1992; Håpnes, Sørensen 1995; Bimber 2000; Stanley 2003) and who are not (sexually) harassed on the Internet (Cherny, Weise, 1996). With the help of the 'script'-concept, questions about whose work, skills, ambitions and needs are supported by technology can be posed, showing how not only in culture but also in technology itself exclusion mechanisms can be incorporated or maintained (Green et al. 1993; Hofmann 1999; Rommes et al. 1999; Rommes 2002a; Bardini, Horvath 1995).

The liberal feminist tradition and especially policies based on this research framework have been criticized for unconsciously replicating the male norm in society: if all barriers are removed, women should become as active and in the same way active as men. Although material preconditions and resources are indeed vital for the inclusion of many (but certainly not all) women, the relevance and the pleasure of IT use for individual women need to be clear before strategies based on these models may work, which brings us to the second research and policy framework.

The main thesis of the *standpoint theory* is that women and 'femininities' (e.g. female connotated characteristics, skills and values) need to be revalued and regarded as equally or even higher valued than male connotated values and skills. Hence, many but not all researchers in this tradition assume that men and women are fundamentally different, either because of biological reasons or by socialization. According to this tradition, both technologies themselves and the cultures surrounding them are not adjusted to 'feminine' requirements, such as relevant content, utilitarian rather then fun functionalities or education and training based on 'feminine' learning styles. By making IST more relevant for women, women will automatically find it more attractive and may even informally learn the skills they need to include themselves in the Information Society. Hence, inclusion initiatives based on this research framework can be described as following the 'rational non-use model', as they assume that women's lack of interest for IST is the result of rational choices by women, and inclusion is achieved by changing IST, rather than by requiring women to change. This policy framework is presently common amongst private and commercial companies and inclusion initiatives whose aim is, amongst others, to create a larger market by designing more diversified games, software and other products and targeting women as buyers or consumers of IST. Presently, this framework is also common amongst managers of companies who want to attract and retain women in the IT industry in order to have employees with better communicative or social skills, or who, as they are women, "know their female consumers better". Gender studies scholars have criticized this assumption extensively for essentializing 'women'.

Nowadays, among researchers within this tradition it is more common not to write about 'women', but rather about e.g. 'people with feminine connotated interests', as masculine and feminine connotated preferences, skills and characteristics can be found amongst both men and women. Indeed, several researchers have shown that introducing more women as designers or program-mers does not necessarily result in products better geared towards women (Sørensen 1992; Rommes 2002b), nor that female IT professionals are more communicative (Faulkner 2006). Rather, design processes are needed in which the designer-standpoint and its commonalities and differences with user-standpoints are made explicit, independent of who the designers and users are. Moreover, an often-heard phrase within this tradition is that technologies need to be attractive for a wider diversity of users, including those with feminine connotated interests, values or characteristics.

The main disadvantage of strategies based on the standpoint epistemology, especially if 'women' and 'feminine connotated interests' are regarded as the same, is that by working with these stereotypes they are being reinforced. By designing for so-called 'female values' (e.g. 'simple' interfaces or products aimed to teach girls to become relationship- and fashion-oriented women) we reinforce existing stereotypes and produce gendered subjects (Cassell, Jenkins 1998). This criticism applies equally to such optimistic accounts as those followed by cyberfeminists who point at the great potential of IST to improve women's lives because of its communicative potential, but who reinforce dualist gender accounts at the same time. The third research framework tries to find a way out of this stereotypical, dichotomous way of thinking by arguing that both IST and conceptions of gender need to change.

By far the most researchers within gender and IST studies nowadays identify themselves as working in the *post-structuralist* research framework. This tradition was inspired by the cultural turn in gender and technology research in the 90s and led to more interest in how identities or gendered subjectivities are shaped and how language, representations and images influence identity formations. Researchers within this framework refuse 'grand theories' about men/women and masculinities/femininities, as these theories themselves may help in creating and reproducing the symbolic link between masculinity and IT which makes IT a 'gender inauthentic' pursuit for many (but certainly not all) women (see for this argument e.g. Gansmo et al. 2003). Policy makers who follow post-structuralist lines of argument for explaining the gender gap in IST can be seen to follow the image model: they aim to disconnect the symbolic link between technologies and masculinities that is held responsible for the gender gap. To change these images, post-structuralists study the constructed nature of gender, technology and their relations. Both gender and IT are considered to be co-constructed, meaning that they mutually shape each other: masculinity is a defining characteristic of what technology is and 'being fascinated by techno-logies' is a defining characteristic of dominant masculinities in society.

Consequently, gender researchers within this tradition try to symbolically 'deconstruct' and redefine both 'femininity' and 'IT', showing how instable these categories are. This is done, for example, by analyzing the many individual experiences that oppose gender and technology dichotomies or by retracing the semiotic or historical roots of the categories to show how they are the result of contingencies (like e.g. Oldenziel (1999) did with the category 'technology').

Computing science like many other technology fields is about analyzing existing worlds and building artifacts on the basis of these analyses. Gender researchers following a post-structuralist framework inquire: what values are present in society and inscribed in technology? With what kinds of assumptions and values about technology, users and the society do designers work? Whose values and experiences are represented and what dichotomies and stereotypes are repeated in technologies and technological cultures? As argued before, gender researchers are, because of their multi-disciplinary background and simultaneous insider/outsider position, well situated to pose these kinds of questions about (hidden) norms (see also Björkman et al., this volume).

Indeed, several feminist scholars have been questioning the 'norm'al. Schelhowe (2004, 2005), for instance, discusses how computing science itself has been seen and has developed as an academic discipline. She questions the "normality" of seeing computing science as a kind of mathematics or as an engineering discipline, both disciplines with a strong male connotation, and she shows that it could have been otherwise. Similarly, Turkle and Papert (1990) have made visible the paradigms and domination of masculine connotated values in the teaching of computing science whereas Kvande and Faulkner have shown the persistence and dominance of masculine norms within engineering organizations (Faulkner 2000a; Kvande, Rasmussen 1994; Kvande 1999). Researchers have shown how some representations and some values rather than others became incorporated in technologies (Oost 2000; Faulkner 2000b). By studying how the at times hidden norms in education, programming practices and technologies have become dominant, alternatives can be suggested.

For policy-makers and designers, the realization that men and women fall into more than two categories means that there is no single strategy that will work to include 'all women'. Instead of aiming at standardized large systems, designers need to pay attention to local, contextualized knowledge and they need to be aware of the translations that are necessary to move from one context, location and set of knowledge to another (see e.g. Suchman 1994). Rather than encouraging designers to take into account potential users' different access to resources or to turn attention to feminine connotated values, gender researchers within the post-structuralist tradition encourage designers to pay attention to their specific users, to choose adequate design methodologies and to attempt to dissolve the boundaries between designers and users (Sørensen et al., forthcoming; Rommes 2006).

Gender researchers within the post-structuralist framework are mainly interested in the question: what gendered subjects are being (re)produced in work situations, through (in)formal teaching situations or by becoming a user or a designer of technologies? One method of studying this is to analyze biographies of women or female engineers interested in technology (Henwood et al. 2001; Herman, Ellen 2004) or to study the interactions between designers that may lead to gendered design choices (Oudshoorn et al. 2004). Another method is to closely study the gendered interactions in classrooms that may lead to gendered interactions with IT (Volman 1997; Stepulevage 2001). Similarly, interactions between IST and the users have been studied, to clarify the agency users have in adopting gendered technologies and to create more awareness for plural and diverse experiences. Several books have recently been published on how technologies are incorporated in everyday life at home (e.g. Berker et al. 2006; Lie 2003; Rohracher 2005).

Our conclusion is that gender studies as a whole have gained something from each perspective on gender and IT. From liberal feminism we have learned to pay attention to women: where are they, why are they excluded, what barriers do they encounter, in what ways are their lives being supported (or not) by technology? From standpoint theory we learned to look for feminine connotated values: in what kind of society do we want to live, what values and priorities are being supported by technologies and the technological culture and what hidden norms shape ourselves and our society? And from post-structuralism we have learned the importance of language, of deconstructing the values and dicho- tomies that are presented as given, the importance of gender identity formations and how gender and technology co-construct each other.

Although we have defined researchers as belonging to one or the other tradition, this does not necessarily mean that they would place themselves in that tradition or that their work solely or even comfortably fits within the traditions in which we have placed them. The division we have made is meant to show how diverse gender research approaches to IST can be, and the reader can find elements of each research framework throughout the various chapters in this book. In practice, most researchers, just as the authors here, have been inspired by and have adopted elements from several research frameworks, which is also the reason why we have not tried to place the contributions within the frameworks.

Clearly, gender studies encompass a multitude of approaches, disciplines and methods. What, especially in the past, has been common and specific about women's studies has been its close relation of theoretical analyses with political aims of facilitating changes in society to improve the position of women. However, as gender studies gradually became embedded in academia, its emphasis has shifted towards analytical, deconstructive research questions, which are relevant for changing society.[4] Such gender studies approaches run the risk of sticking with the mere analysis of how technologies 'could have been made otherwise', without being able to offer alternatives.

This book is the result of combining a gender studies perspective with a computing science perspective. Computing science implies focusing on the construction of technologies and on how to change society by (re)building information technology. In the combination of computing science and gender studies the authors of the chapters in this book have tried to be critical while at

---

4   The renaming of women's studies to 'gender studies' is important in this respect: the focus has shifted from improving the position of women towards analyzing the way gender (mascu- linities and femininities), often combined with other axes of diversity and inequality such as ethnicities, race, age and sexualities, is constructed in society on various levels.

the same time constructive and proactive in formulating alternatives. But first we turn to the field of socially oriented software design as a subfield of computing science to find out about its specific traditions, perspectives and methodologies and to explore in what ways gender research fits with it.

3   Socially Oriented Software Design

At first glance computing science does not seem to invite cooperation or easily integrate with gender research. In this section we will review the historical emergence of the field of socially oriented software design, a subfield of computing science that most easily lends itself to being combined with perspectives from gender studies[5], and we will point out the relations to gender research.

Software development[6] is a central issue in computing science. It generally proceeds in a sequence of phases, starting with requirements analysis. Here the structure and the present situation of a particular application area, the goals and needs of the actors and stakeholders are assessed and analyzed, and the necessary software functionality is determined. Most gender research referring to software development introduced gender as an additional analytic aspect to characterize contexts and actors. In the subsequent more constructive phases the software concept is specified and described in increasing detail and formality, finally leading to the implementation of a program in a concrete socio-technical environment. Much less gender research has been done with respect to the constructive phases.

The socially oriented approach to software design places particular emphasis on understanding the organizational and social context of the software development process and the use of software, comparable to what has become known as 'human-centred systems design' in Scandinavia and the UK (Pain et al. 1993). Scientists and practitioners who represent this approach develop and use methods and description techniques that allow for an intense involvement of the later software users in requirements analysis and in the development and evaluation of design ideas.

In the early years of computer construction and use, computers were exclusively used by scientists from the 'exact' sciences, like mathematics or physics, who programmed the machines for their own use. In their programs they dealt with problems already formalized (mostly mathematical calculations) or modeled problems and processes that were relevant and well understood in their

---

5   This is not to say that there are no other candidate fields.
6   'Software development' and 'software design' are often used as synonyms. In the context of 'analysis and design', 'design' denotes the more constructive later phases of software development.

scientific contexts. If their programs would not work or if the results seemed unlikely, these programmers knew well what they had wanted to model and to achieve and they were able to eliminate their own errors.

In the 1970s, the early time of interactive computing, computers were introduced to more and more fields of society and non-computer experts increasingly started using software for their daily work. Systems were designed for them – users and designers became two separate groups with different professional backgrounds and expertise. Often in human-computer interaction, users did not know what they were allowed to type in and what the subsequent output meant. In cases of malfunction they had to wait for experts to help them. They often experienced computer use as complicated and annoying and not very helpful for their professional tasks. Users wished interaction to be more 'user-friendly'; the academic field of 'human-computer interaction (HCI)' was formed (for overviews see Myers 1998, Maass 1993).

Graphical user interfaces as we know them today were expected to diminish these problems. The new interaction paradigm, 'direct manipulation' of 'objects' in 'windows', had been developed in cooperation between computing scientists and cognitive scientists taking into consideration what was known about human perception, thinking and learning (Shneiderman 1983). In fact these interfaces required less specific knowledge and skills about computers. Software developers started to distinguish between 'naïve users' (meaning *computer-naïve*), 'occasional' and 'expert users'. In order to help naïve users, software use was made as simple as possible. This may be quite convenient for users, but also keeps them from learning more about how the computer works or how they can use application programs in more sophisticated ways.

A technical system that is to facilitate human work not only must be usable but also useful or 'task-adequate' in the sense that its functionality has to match the tasks to be accomplished. Software design has become an important part of work design in that it shapes work processes - it enables or interferes with them. Software not only incorporates assumptions about users and their work but also mirrors the designer's respect for that work. Gender stereotypes concerning work done by women can lead to inadequate software design. The resulting product may simplify the tasks, thereby reducing the necessary competences and preventing workers from extending their skills. It may even fail to support the workers' jobs and make it more difficult for them to reach their goals (cf. Jeanette Hofmann's early studies of word processing systems, Hofmann 1999).

In office work a lot of relevant work activities may remain unseen by observers: communication and interaction work that is mostly done by female office workers is considered as just requiring their 'natural female' skills and no serious education. Outsiders like systems analysts may easily overlook or undervalue these aspects of work (Webster 1993; an example case is described by Maass and Rommes, this volume). Systems design based on such patchy analysis is prone to be task-inadequate, it risks either to make work more complicated by the software or to keep users in place with overly simple task models and thus to reproduce a gender-specific division of labor.

In the 1980s the European trade unions called for more workplace democracy and user participation in technology design and introduction. The first participatory projects started in Scandinavia and Germany (Bjerknes, Bratteteig 1994). At that time in particular the German-speaking 'Software-Ergonomie' research community (the equivalent to the Anglo-American HCI-community) started to cooperate with work scientists to make sure that software design did not interfere with good work design.

Mainstream software practitioners who did not follow the socially oriented approach often were surprised by the fact that the users of their systems were not content and were reluctant to use the systems. The dominant software development practices with their traditional emphasis on formal analysis and description techniques that designers regarded as 'neutral' or 'objective' turned out to be inappropriate as they were unintentionally biased. Systems did not fit the users' expectations and needs because, without being aware of it, the designers had assumed that future users would have the same abilities and preferences as they did and had designed for people like themselves ("I-methodology", cf. Akrich 1995; Rommes et al. 1999). Critical scientists from software engineering as well as from HCI were confirmed in their view that good software cannot be developed by software experts alone. They called for more communication between designers and 'end users', so software designers could better understand the particular area of business and work their software would be applied to.

This directed more attention to the practices of requirements analysis. Various new 'participatory' methods were developed or appropriated from other fields, in particular from anthropology in order to investigate users' tasks and needs (Blomberg et al. 2003). Prominent software companies started to include anthropologists in their research teams and used their field methods of enquiry. The users' application knowledge and work experience that tend to stay invisible with traditional analysis methods were discovered as crucial resources for good design; they need to be acquired by means of qualitative interviews and observational studies (cf. Suchman 1995). This new and respectful attitude constitutes a significant shift in the relationship between design and use, putting an end to the traditional higher esteem for design activities in comparison to use activities.

Due to their different professional backgrounds, designers and users have no common set of representation techniques. A lot of 'participatory design' research addresses the question of what kinds of representations or descriptions can facilitate a balanced, respectful and productive user-designer communication and cooperation and thus the empowerment of users in design. Michael Muller (2003: 1054) points out that the general concern of HCI research is "to bridge between two spaces – the world of software professionals, and the world of end-users". In his survey article he characterizes recently developed participatory design methods that fall in the "hybrid realm" between the distinct work domains of developers and users as an attempt to create a "third space". Such third spaces "contain an unpredictable and changing combination of attributes of each of the two bordering spaces", Muller explains, referring to cultural theory (ibid.: 1053, Bhabha 1994). Cooperative workshops will "introduce novel procedures that are not part of conventional work practices" of either party (Muller 2003: 1056). Storytelling techniques are conducive to the formulation of individual experiences and perspectives and allow compact and yet comprehensible descriptions and stimulate discussions. Design games serve as levelers as they put all group members under the same rules of play and enhance joyful communication among them. The cooperative creation of descriptive artifacts promotes the mutual exploration of positions and approaches, resolution of conflicts and combination of views. Taking heterogeneity as the norm, 'third spaces' further mutual learning, the challenging of assumptions, and the formation of new ideas. The concept of 'third space' and the various mentioned attributes and aims indicate a close affinity between participatory design methods and gender research approaches which call for a crossing of boundaries, the look from various perspectives and the reflection of silent assumptions.

Cooperation with users in the analysis and construction phases allows designers to discover and describe work processes in detail and to investigate and specify what system characteristics are desirable from the workers' points of view. As opposed to such participatory methods, traditional computing science methods are based on the assumption that structures and procedures which are to be supplemented or substituted by a software system can be identified 'objectively' by means of formal methods and with minimal direct user contact. Computing science is firmly rooted in the positivist tradition of natural sciences and the development of formal descriptions for objects and processes is a core issue. Software developers are trained to use and produce descriptions at various levels of abstraction; a software program is only the last step in a row of abstractions. In order to develop a program that automates or supports work activities in some area, developers have to make out the relevant elements und structures underlying and surrounding these processes. For a long time, the dominant assumption in computing science was that structures in our world are 'given' or 'real', so software developers just need to 'discover' them and then build a 'correct' model in their software. This myth of objectivity has often been criticized, not only by feminist science and technology researchers but also from inside computing science.

Christiane Floyd, one of the early proponents of participatory design in Germany, suggests a "new understanding of science" in her introduction to the book "Software Development and Reality Construction" (Floyd et al. 1992): "It embodies an awareness of how the observer constructs reality by the act of observation, how the questions we ask influence the answers we get and how we interpret them" (Floyd 1992: 19). In her opinion "an important aspect of computer science is that it deals with *creating reality*: the technical reality of the programs executed on the computer, and the conditions for the human reality which unfolds around the computer in use" (Floyd 1992: 20, original emphasis). This human reality, we would like to add, is structured by gender relations and technical systems have consequences for gender relations.

Instead of relying on the traditional categories 'right' and 'wrong', Floyd continues, good quality in software development and use requires that we "go beyond them by finding categories for expressing *the felicity of our choices*, for distinguishing ,more or less desirable' as we proceed in making distinctions and decisions in communal design processes" (ibid.). Contrary to the myth of objectivity we must see software construction as happening in a social context, shaped by viewpoints, interests and power structures, and the resulting product as depending on who is involved.

Developers have to carefully reflect their own positions in a world that is – among other factors like class, ethnicity or age – structured by gender. Without this, products may turn out to be unconsciously biased (see above "I-methodology"), unusable and task-inadequate. Thus software development can benefit from gender research. A combination of insights into gender issues on a theoretical level (e.g. gender-specific division of labor, gender connotated values and skills and gendered identity concepts), detailed studies of users and use contexts as well as direct involvement of users in the design (participatory design) will help designers in the construction phases to make decisions that explicitly take up and shape social reality, including gender relations. Such decisions may lead to Information Society Technology that supports and empowers a diversity of users.

4   Gender Research and Computing Science: Combining Deconstruction, Construction and Empowerment

The current transformation process towards the Information Society relies on the use of information technology not only by institutions but also by all citizens. Society in general is gendered and so is the Information Society, as we pointed out. Information technology itself plays an important role in enabling or preventing equal participation. Choices made in software design immediately influence the possible uses and the necessary user skills: they affect work and educational processes. Participatory strategies are being introduced into mainstream software development practices as taught in computing science to better meet users' needs and interests. As gender research has shown, gender relations shape and are shaped by the material world around us, and increasingly software forms a part of that world.

As described in section 2, gender research in the field of technology has been done from various perspectives. It has focused on analysis and deconstruction rather than on constructing alternative software programs. How can gender research actually inspire concrete software construction and lead to an empowerment of formerly excluded groups? As modeling decisions are not only determined by rules and technical necessities but also follow social preferences and interests, gender research can inform technology construction by particularly making software designers aware of their own (gendered) social assumptions and of the social consequences of the technology they create. So they will be able to critically reflect and adjust their assumptions or at least make conscious and explicit assumptions.

However, there seems to be a methodological gulf between gender research and computing science, between gender analysis and traditional software development, and deconstruction and construction that makes the transfer of results quite difficult. While post-structuralist gender research tries to open up categories and challenge distinctions, technology construction needs clear categories. This is particularly true for traditional requirements analysis that mainly focuses on formal modeling, but on the way from requirements analysis to some final system any informal models at some point have to be transformed into formal models with well-defined constituents and behaviors, filtering out 'irrelevant' details, irregularities and variety. At this point gender research has to make sure that gender aspects are perceived as relevant without essentializing gender.

Liberal feminism draws the attention to the particular situation of women; research from standpoint theory, too, works with rather clear-cut categories of masculinity and femininity. Hence it is not surprising that designers have mainly (if at all) used the insights from those research frameworks (see Rommes 2006). But, as discussed in section 2, by doing this, they run the risk of essentializing either women or IST; of either reinforcing gender stereotypes or forcing women (or those who do not fit the norm incorporated in technologies) to change, educate themselves or stay out. Post-structuralist gender research has clearly shown that the fixation on 'what it means to be male or female' reduces people's options and cuts down on their freedom of action while leaving dominant gender structures in society intact.

Post-structuralist analysis, however, goes very well together with participatory design approaches. Researchers and practitioners of socially oriented software design have already opened up the traditional view of software development by putting forth user-oriented criteria for good software quality (usability, task-adequacy), criteria that cannot be formally applied but must be interpreted for every particular context, and new non-formal (participatory) techniques to involve the later users in analysis and construction. Similarly, post-structuralist gender researchers avoid categorizations, they rather focus on how these categories are constructed and hence can be avoided. One of the main points of post-structuralist researchers is that 'designing for all women' is not possible, but rather that designers need to study each particular application context. Techniques adopted from socially oriented software design can be very suitable for this as well as empowering for the women involved, as will be demonstrated by several chapters in this book (see also Kreutzner, Schelhowe 2003).

The various approaches to gender research presented above provide starting points for a critical assessment and an improvement of technology design in the sense that they allow for equal opportunities in the Information Society. Interest in gender research hopefully will rise, as the official directives for publicly funded research (like in the EU Research Framework Programs and IST programs) require scientists to include gender in their research projects.

We intend to explore and exemplify the relations between gender research and software design and thereby inspire innovation as well as further research. The case studies presented in this book will show how gender research can lead to gender-sensitive software construction, how conventional software design could have been improved by applying gender research, but also that basic aims of gender research, like the dissolution of fixed categories, are challenged by the necessity of formal determination in software construction.

The book brings together theory and practice of gender research and computing science and explores their mutual relevance. The interaction of gender and computing science is explored on several levels: first, analyzing IST design and scientific innovation processes from a deconstructionist view; second, describing and analyzing the rationale of concrete construction processes and software products; and third, showing the relevance of both for technical education and empowerment.

Summarizing the Chapters

As a start, and complementing this introduction, *Heike Jensen*'s article on the World Summit of Information Society WSIS focuses our attention on the relevance of information technology in the global design of the Information Society. Jensen asks whose policies are represented in the visions and the planning process. She analyzes power structures between men and women in the decision-making process of WSIS and finds that these prevent the discussion of issues that would promote equality.

In **part II "Analysis and Deconstruction"** the specific standpoint of researchers of both gender and IST is explored and exploited for a critical analysis of society and information technology. The authors of the first two chapters apply critical gender-analytical perspectives to some of today's highly visible fields of innovation. The authors of the third chapter reflect on their own working conditions as gender researchers inside computing science.

Jutta Weber and Corinna Bath analyze how computing science scholars infuse their creations such as robots and software agents with 'sociality' or 'emotionality'. They show that in order to make machines appear social or emotional, computing scientists utilize gender stereotypes. As they construct the 'future' by designing technological innovations, these scientists perpetuate existing social and emotional characteristics of humans in their most reduced and standardized forms. Are computing scientists creating a world in which humans one day will be forced to stick to even more confining standards of social and gendered behavior than today?

Cecile Crutzen analyzes and critiques developments in the field of ambient intelligence where networked devices surround humans, register their presence and actions, and react even before a person realizes that her environment needs to change. Crutzen argues that the space needed for interaction with the technology – what she calls "transformative critical rooms" – will disappear in such scenarios. How will gender be interpreted by such 'intelligent' devices, will they again stabilize the existing fixed meanings of gender?

Christina Björkman, Pirjo Elovaara and Lena Trojer discuss their positions at the boundaries between disciplines as well as at the boundary between the inside and the outside of academic knowledge production. They reflect on the new turn in feminist technoscience from analysis and deconstruction to intervention and construction. In their own research they are hindered by, and at the same time challenge, the boundaries they encounter. They conclude the chapter with a list of the potentials and challenges of feminist technoscience research.

In **part III "Construction of Information Society Technology"** software systems are analyzed that have been unconsciously gendered and alternatives are discussed. The chapters provide case studies for how gender research can inform and inspire design processes. The authors demonstrate how gender research in computing science can move from deconstruction and critique to gender-conscious software construction.

Susanne Maass and Els Rommes give an example of how gender research can be used to improve software products and software-supported work processes. They analyze call center software and find that unconscious gender stereotypes have guided the design and now interfere with call center agents' service work in customer interaction. Crucial and gendered aspects of the agents' work have remained invisible to the designers. The analysis instruments, too, need a critical revision in order to become applicable to a wider diversity of work contexts. Based on their gender analysis, the authors suggest modifications of the software to make it more task-adequate.

Tanja Carstensen and Gabriele Winker look at women's organizations' uses of and needs for information technology and analyze them from a gender perspective. They present a case in which they themselves set up a database of women's projects and implemented tools to search it and to add further feminist projects. They describe the conceptualization phase, design phase, and users' reactions. The case study exemplifies the problem of combining construction and de-construction: their software design required to find clear categories for the database, the heterogeneous feminist groups for which it was designed, however, would have preferred to avoid restrictive categorization, as this is currently much discussed in post-structuralist debates.

Tanja Paulitz provides an analysis of the procedures and results of two design projects, one incorporating unconscious gender stereotypes and one paying attention to gender research results. She explains how and where both strategies affected the success of the designed systems and suggests how the first project could have gained from explicitly applying a gender perspective.

In **part IV "Education and Empowerment for the Information Society"** the interaction of specific information technologies with people and their lives is discussed. While in the chapters above authors discuss the necessity of gender-sensitive design processes, the authors in this part have tried to improve technologies and developed teaching material to make software and teaching practices more empowering. Several case-studies are presented in which educational aspects of software design and technical aspects of teaching practices are discussed.

Ruth Meßmer and Sigrid Schmitz study gender in e-learning scenarios. They describe a method of teaching technology courses for mixed groups of computing science students and gender studies students. They argue that the method helps the computing science students as future IST designers to understand the impact of gender categories and to develop some degree of gender-sensitivity. At the same time, gender studies students gain insights into the implementation of design decisions in technology. Both groups of students seem to have taught each other. The authors outline the characteristics of these courses and describe processes and interactions they observed.

Edeltraud Hanappi-Egger developed a computer game that mirrors the fact that life and the world are gendered and invisibly determine people's options and decisions. The game is made for children, especially for girls, and allows them to simulate important decisions in a girl's course of life (e.g. leave school, get pregnant) and to experience the consequences of their decisions. Besides the fun of playing it, the aim of the game is to create realistic situations that make the users reflect on their gendered lives.

Bettina Munk provides an example of technology construction that is inspired by gender research results. She assumes that offering girls more appealing computer games can help raise their interest in computing science. Based on an analysis of girls' media interests and media use an educational cell-phone software geared towards these interests was developed that teaches basic programming concepts and procedures. Munk suggests this as a way to combine technology experience with fun for girls.

Susann Hartmann, Heike Wiesner and Andreas Wiesner-Steiner present robotics as a field that can provide children with technological design experience. They analyze the effects of robotics workshops on girls' technology interests and career visions. The authors find that the technical robotics material itself is gendered and has an impact on the gendering of group dynamics and on 'doing gender' during the workshop. Designing and programming robots turned out to raise girls' anticipation of a technical profession if both, course concepts and technologies, were gender-sensitive.

Although the authors are from various disciplines and use different research frameworks, they all share some basic questions: What are gender aspects in IST development? Why should gender be integrated in analysis and design? And how can this be done? A gender perspective on IST serves as an eye-opener to study power structures, symbolic attributions and individual inequalities in society. Together, the chapters in this book show that many decisions in designing a course, in developing a technology or in constructing society are (unconsciously) gendered. They illustrate that developers, teachers and policy makers do have choices and they can choose to make a difference.

We hope that our diverse readers will feel inspired and encouraged to include gender in their research, teaching and development practices. Only with conscious attention to gender issues a "people-centered, inclusive and development-oriented Information Society" as claimed in the WSIS Declaration[7] can be achieved.

---

7   See footnote 1.

References

Akrich, Madeleine (1995): User Representations: Practices, Methods and Sociology. In: Rip, Arie; Misa, Thomas J.; Schot, John (eds.): Managing Technology in Society. The Approach of Constructive Technology Assessment. London/New York: Pinter: 167-184.

Bardini, Thierry; Horvath, August T. (1995): The Social Construction of the Personal Computer User. In: Journal of Communication 45(3): 40-65.

Berker, Thomas; Hartmann, Marit; Punie, Yves; Ward, Katie (eds.) (2006): Domestication of Media and Technology. Berkshire: Open University Press, McGraw-Hill Education.

Bhabha, Homi K. (1994) The Location of Culture. London: Routledge.

Bimber, Bruce (2000): Measuring the Gender Gap on the Internet. In: Social Science Quarterly 81(3): 868-876.

Bjerknes, Gro; Bratteteig, Tone (1994): User Participation: A Strategy for Work Life Democracy? In: Trigg, Randy; Anderson, Susan I.; Dykstra-Erickson, Elizabeth A. (eds.): PDC'94: Proceedings of the Participatory Design Conference, CPSR: 3-12.

Blomberg, Jeanette; Burrell, Mark; Guest, Greg (2003): The Ethnographic Approach to Design. In: Jacko, Julie A.; Sears, Andrew (eds.): 964-986.

Bowker, Geoffrey C.; Star, Susan Leigh (2000): Sorting things out; classification and its consequences. Cambridge/Massachusetts/London: MIT Press.

Cassell, Justine; Jenkins, Henry (1998): Chess for Girls? Feminism and Computer Games. In: Cassell, Justine; Jenkins, Henry (eds.): From Barbie to Mortal Kombat - Gender and Computer Games. Cambridge/London: MIT Press: 2-45.

Cherny, Lynn; Weise, Elisabeth R. (eds.) (1996): Wired_Women - gender and new realities in cyberspace. Seattle: Seal Press.

Cockburn, Cynthia (1985): Machinery of Dominance; Women, men and technical knowhow. London/Sydney/Dover/New Hampshire: Pluto Press.

Eriksson, Inger V.; Kitchenham, Barbara A.; Tijdens, Kea G. (eds.) (1991): Women, work, and computerization: understanding and overcoming bias in work and education: Proceedings of the IFIP TC9/WG 9.1 Conference, Helsinki, Finland, 30 June-2 July 1991. Amsterdam: North Holland.

Faulkner, Wendy (2000a): Dualisms, Hierarchies and Gender in Engineering. In: Social Studies of Science 30(5): 759-792.

Faulkner, Wendy (2000b): The Power and the Pleasure? A Research Agenda for "Making Gender Stick" to Engineers. In: Science, Technology & Human Values 25(1): 87-119.

Faulkner, Wendy (2006): Gender in/of engineering; a research report. Edinburgh: Economic & Social Research Council.

Floyd, Christiane (1992): Human Questions in Computer Science. In: Floyd et al. (1992): 15-27.

Floyd, Christiane; Züllighoven, Heinz; Budde, Reinhard; Keil-Slawik, Reinhard (eds.) (1992): Software Development and Reality Construction. Berlin: Springer.

Gansmo, Helen J.; Lagesen, Vivian A.; Sørensen, Knut Holtan (2003): Forget the hacker? A critical re-appraisal of Norwegian studies of gender and ICT. In: Lie (2003): 34-68.

Green, Eileen; Owen, Jenny; Pain, Den (eds.) (1993): Gendered by Design? Information Technology and Office Systems. London/Washington: Taylor & Francis.

Hacker, Sally (1989): Pleasure, power and technology: some tales of gender, engineering, and the cooperative workplace. Boston: Unwin Hyman.

Haddon, Lesley (1992): Explaining ICT consumption; The case of the home computer. In: Silverstone, Roger; Hirsch, Ernst (eds.): Consuming Technologies. Media and Information in Domestic Spaces. London/New York: Routledge: 82-96.

Hales, Mike (1993): Human-centred systems, gender and computer supported cooperative work. In: Probert, Wilson (1993): 101-125.

Håpnes, Tove; Sørensen, Knut Holtan (1995): Competition and Collaboration in Male Shaping of Computing: A study of a Norwegian Hacker Culture. In: Grint, Keith; Gill, Rosalind (eds.), The Gender-Technology Relation. London/Bristol: Taylor & Francis: 174-191.

Henwood, Flis; Hughes, G.; Kennedy, Helen; Miller, Nod; Wyatt, Sally (2001): Cyborg lives in context: Writing women's technobiographies. In: Henwood, Flis; Kennedy, Helen & Miller, Nod (eds.): Cyborg Lives? Women's Technobiographies.York: Raw Nerve Books: 11-34.

Herman, Clem; Ellen, Debbie (2004): "I would say I've fallen into IT": Career paths of women network technicians participating in the JIVE project. Paper presented at the Gender and ICT Symposium: Brussels 20th Jan 2004, Brussels.

Hofmann, Jeanette (1999): Writers, Texts and Writing Acts - Constructed Realities in Word Processing Software. In: MacKenzie, Donald; Wajcman, Judy (eds.): The Social Shaping of Technology. Buckingham: Open University Press: 222-243.

Jacko, Julie A.; Sears, Andrew (eds.) (2003): The Human-Computer Interaction Handbook: Fundamentals, Evolving Technologies, and Emerging Applications. Mahwah, N.J.: Lawrence Erlbaum.

Kreutzner, Gabriele; Schelhowe, Heidi (eds.) (2003): Agents of Change. Virtuality, Gender, and the Challenge to Traditional University. Opladen: Leske + Budrich 2003.

Kvande, Elin (1999): 'In the Belly of the Beast' - Constructing Femininities in Engineering Organizations. In: The European Journal of Women's Studies 6(3): 202-230.

Kvande, Elin; Rasmussen, Bente (1994): Men in male-dominated organizations and their encounter with women intruders. In: Scandinavian Journal of Management 10(2): 163-173.

Lie, Merete. (ed.) (2003): He, She and IT Revisited; New Perspectives on Gender in the Information Society. Oslo: Gyldendal Norsk Forlag.

Maass, Susanne (1993): Software-Ergonomie. Benutzer- und aufgabenorientierte Systemgestaltung. In: Informatik-Spektrum 16(4): 191-205.

Marcus, Aaron; West Gould, Emilie (2000): Crosscurrents – Cultural Dimensions and Global Web User-Interface Design. In: Interactions 7(4): 32-46.

Muller, Michael J. (2003): Participatory Design: The Third Space in HCI. In: Jacko, Sears, (eds.) (2003): 1051-1068.

Myers, Brad A. (1998): A Brief History of Human Computer Interaction Technology. In: Interactions 5(2): 44-54.

N., Veena (sic!); Zorn, Isabel; Schelhowe, Heidi; Draude, Claude; Büschenfeldt, Maika (2004): GIST: Gender Perspectives Increasing Diversity for Information Society. In: Gender, Technology and Development. (8)3: 440-443.

Nielsen Netratings (2001). Internet Audiences by Gender. quoted from: Michael Pastore: Internet remains a Men's Domain. http://www.clickz.com/stats/sectors/demographics/article.php/5901_809341#table (Last access 2006-07-25).

OECD 2006, Organisation for Economic Co-operation and Development - Global Science Forum (2006). Evolution of Student Interest in Science and Technology Studies. Policy Report http://www.oecd.org/dataoecd/16/30/36645825.pdf (Last access 2006-06-19).

Oldenziel, Ruth (1997): Boys and Their Toys: The Fisher Body Craftsman's Guild, 1930-1968, and the Making of a Male Technical Domain. In: Technology and Culture 38(1): 60-98.

Oldenziel, Ruth (1999): Making Technology Masculine; Men, women and modern machines in America 1870-1945. Amsterdam: Amsterdam University Press.

Oost, Ellen C. J. v. (1998): Aligning Gender and New Technology: the case of early administrative automation. In: Disco, Cornelius & Meulen, Bernard v. d. (eds.): Getting New Technologies Together: Studies in Making Sociotechnical Order. Berlin: Walter de Gruyter: 179-203.

Oost, Ellen C. J. v. (2000): Making the computer masculine. In: Balka, Ellen; Smith, Richard (eds.): Women, Work and Computerization, Charting a Course to the Future. Dordrecht: Kluwer Academic Publishers: 9-16.

Oudshoorn, Nelly; Rommes, Els; Stienstra, Marcelle (2004): Configuring the User as Everybody. Gender and Design in Information and Communication Technologies. In: Science, Technology & Human Values 29(1): 30-63.

Pain, Den; Owen, Jenny; Franklin, Ian; Green, Eileen (1993): Human-Centred Systems Design: A Review of Trends within the Broader Systems Development Context. In: Green et al. (2003): 11-30.

Probert, Belinda; Wilson, Bruce W. (eds.) (1993): Pink Collar Blues. Work, Gender and Technology. Melbourne University Press.

Rasmussen, Bente; Hapnes, Tove (1991): Excluding Women from the Technologies of the Future? A case study of the culture of computer science. In: Futures 23(10): 1107-1119.

Rohracher, Harald (ed.). (2005): User Involvement in Innovation Processes; Strategies and Limitations from a Socio-Technical Perspective (Vol. 44). München, Wien: Profil Verlag.

Rommes, Els (2002a): Gender Scripts and the Internet; The Design and Use of Amsterdam's Digital City. Enschede: Twente University.

Rommes, Els (2002b). Worlds Apart: Exclusion-processes in DDS. In: Tanabe, Makoto; Besselaar, Peter v. d.; Ishida, Toru (eds.): Digital Cities II; Computational and Sociological Approaches (Vol. LNCS 2362) Berlin/Heidelberg: Springer: 219-232.

Rommes, Els (2006). Gender sensitive design practices. In: Trauth, Eileen M. (ed.): Encyclopedia of Gender and Information Technology. Hershey, Penns.: Idea Group: 675-681.

Rommes, Els; Oost, Ellen C. J.; Oudshoorn, Nelly (1999): Gender in the Design of a Digital City. In: Information Technology, Communication and Society 2(4): 476-495.

Schelhowe, Heidi (2004): Paradigms of Computing Science: The Necessity for Methodological Diversity. In: Gender, Technology and Development (8)3: 321-334.

Schelhowe, Heidi (2005): Gender Questions and Computing Science. In: Morell, Claudia; Sanders, Jo (eds.): Proceedings of the international symposium on Women and ICT: creating global transformation. New York, USA: ACM Press Proceeding Series Vol. 126. Article No. 10. http://portal.acm.org/citation.cfm?id=1117427&coll=portal&dl =ACM&CFID=867154&CFTOKEN=68308085 (Last Access: 2006-09-14).

Schelhowe, Heidi; Vosseberg, Karin (1991): Aspects of Women's Research in Computer Science. In: Eriksson et al. (1991): 67-80.

Shneiderman, Ben (1983): Direct Manipulation. A Step Beyond Programming Languages. In: IEEE Computer 16(8): 57-69.

Sørensen, Knut Holtan (1992): Towards a Feminized Technology? Gendered Values in the Construction of Technology. In: Social Studies of Science 22(1): 5-31.

Sørensen, Knut Holtan; Rommes, Els; Faulkner, Wendy (forthcoming): Technologies of Inclusion; Bridging the Gender Gap in the Information Society.

Stanley, Laura D. (2003): Beyond Access: Psychosocial Barriers to Computer Literacy. In: The Information Society 19: 407-416.

Star, Susan Leigh (1991): Invisible work and silenced dialogues in knowledge representation. In: Eriksson et al. (1991): 81-92.

Stepulevage, Linda (2001): Gender/Technology Relations: complicating the gender binary. In: Gender and Education 13(3): 325-338.

Stewart, James (2002): Information Society, the Internet and Gender: A Summary of Pan-European Statistical Data, Document Number: D02_Part2, Available at: http://www.rcss.ed.ac.uk/sigis/public/D02/D02_Part2.pdf (Last access 2006-07-29).

Suchman, Lucy (1994): Working Relations of Technology Production and Use. In: Computer Supported Cooperative Work (CSCW) 2: 21-39.

Suchman, Lucy (1995): Making Work Visible. In: Communications of the ACM 38(9): 56-64.

Sutton, Rosemary E. (1991): Equity and computers in the schools - a decade of research. In: Review of educational research 61(4): 475-503.

TNS infratest (2006). (N)Onliner Atlas 2006 – Eine Topographie des Digitalen Grabens durch Deutschland http://www.nonliner-atlas.de/pdf/dl_NONLINER-Atlas2006.pdf (Last accessed: 2006-07-25).

Turkle, Sherry; Papert, Seymour (1990): Epistemological Pluralism: Styles and Voices within the Computer Culture. In: Signs: Journal of Women in Culture and Society 16(1): 128-157.

Volman, Monique (1997): Gender-related effects of computer and information literacy education. In: Journal of Curriculum Studies 29(3): 315-328.

Wajcman, Judy (2004). TechnoFeminism. Cambridge, UK ; Malden, MA: PolityPress.

Webster, Juliet (1993): Women's skills and word processors. Gender issues in the development of the automated office. In: Probert, Wilson (1993): 41-59.

Acknowledgements

The editors thank the German Ministry of Education and Research and all other partners who have provided financial support for the organization of the International Symposium GIST – Gender Perspectives Increasing Diversity for Information Society Technology 2004. We also thank the University of Bremen for inviting and funding Els Rommes as a visiting professor in 2005/2006 which made the joint work on this book possible.

We are grateful to Kristene Unsworth for the proof reading of this chapter. Finally, our special thanks to Heidi Schelhowe for many inspiring discussions on gender and IT construction.

The United Nations World Summit on the Information Society: Empowering Women as Shapers of the Information Society?

Heike Jensen

The new information and communication technologies (ICTs) have been the driving force of "globalization". This process has led to a worldwide reorganization of fundamental transactions and relationships, including within the division of labor, the financial markets and the knowledge market. Globalization has had direct or indirect impacts on all cultures and societies and as such has affected women's and men's lives profoundly and in manifold ways. The United Nations (UN) acknowledged the importance of ICTs in restructuring the world when in 2001 they decided to hold a World Summit on the Information Society (WSIS). This summit was to articulate a vision of the "Information Society" and steps to bring it about. The UN organization responsible for WSIS was the International Telecommunication Union (ITU), which coordinates global telecom networks and services.

WSIS was comprised of two summit phases and two summit events, one taking place in Geneva, Switzerland in December 2003 and the other in Tunis, Tunisia in November 2005. WSIS has constituted the prime venue for the articulation of a global normative framework for the Information Society, now codified in the four official outcome documents, the Geneva Declaration of Principles, the Geneva Plan of Action, the Tunis Commitment and the Tunis Agenda. These WSIS documents are likely to have decisive implications for ICT-related public policy formulations, development cooperation and other economic relationships within and between world regions.

The WSIS process made it clear that ICTs are a contested political field because they are a source of political and economic power as well as a potential means of empowerment for marginalized regions and groups. From a gender perspective, it is obvious that the female half of the world's population has so far been at a severe disadvantage with respect to ICTs, be it as users, as designers, or as shapers of the economic and political spheres in which ICTs are embedded. So how were these power issues addressed in the context of WSIS? This article will examine this question from within the discipline of Gender Studies in two steps: First, it will analyze the feminist input and political gains at WSIS. These can be summarized as drawing attention to the specific positions of women vis-à-vis ICTs and as mapping some special measures on women's behalf. Here, the category of gender appears quite straightforwardly as that which defines a group of people and their specific social roles, options and restrictions. Second, the feminist input and its political gains will be contextualized in the overall political WSIS agenda. It will be argued that this agenda, while appearing gender-blind, was a deeply gendered one that has privileged and perpetuated hegemonic masculinity. In this context, gender as a category will be traced as an abstract system of power and representation played out in political processes and institutions.

This twofold analysis is meant to contextualize the achievements of progresssive gender politics and their limits at WSIS in a manner that draws attention to the different and complex gendering mechanisms currently at work in a political arena such as WSIS. It is hoped that a clearer understanding of these mechanisms will contribute to an increased sophistication in challenging masculine prerogatives and gender imbalances and in furthering the empowerment of women in the Information Society.

1   Feminist Input for WSIS

For feminist researchers and activists, the crucial first step in engendering the Information Society and its world summit was to embark on a search for "woman", the marginalized or overlooked element in media and ICT policies and development. The subsequent step was to convert the findings regarding the concerns of different groups of women into political recommendations on their behalf. Such an approach is quite common in any new field of gender inquiry and politics, which is usually opened by women and takes women as the main object. This is the case because women as the dominated gender group have a big stake in understanding how their own gender works to subordinate them, so they generally start by analyzing their subordinated positions and voicing demands based on these analyses. Often, men and masculinity remain undertheorized in such a context. Men themselves, meanwhile, can more easily afford to ignore gender as a problematic concept altogether, because it by default works in their favor and hence may not seem to require conscious engagement on their part. As Greig, Kimmel and Lang (2000: 1) put it,

> "The processes that confer privilege on one group and not another are often invisible to those upon whom that privilege is conferred. Thus, not having to think about race is one of the luxuries of being of a dominant race, just as not having to think about gender is one of the patriarchal dividends that men gain from their position in the

gender order. Men tend not to think of themselves as 'gendered' beings, and this is one reason why policy makers and development practitioners, both men and women, often misunderstand or dismiss 'gender' as a women's issue."

The patriarchal dividends mentioned in the above quote benefit all men, but not all men are equally powerful. Connell (1995) in his groundbreaking work on masculinities coined the term "hegemonic masculinity" to designate the ruling status and ruling mechanism of a specific form of masculinity. According to him,

> "Hegemonic masculinity can be defined as the configuration of gender practice which embodies the currently accepted answer to the problem of the legitimacy of patriarchy, which guarantees (or is taken to guarantee) the dominant position of men and the subordination of women." (Connell 1995: 77)

Hegemonic masculinity thus legitimizes patriarchy and simultaneously normalizes it. Consequently, both patriarchy and hegemonic masculinity to an extent become shielded from scrutiny and questioning, to the effect that even feminist researchers and gender equality advocates may squarely focus their work on girls and women without paying due attention to the intricate gender relationships within and between the genders. Thus the history of gender equality politics has come to be almost synonymous with women's politics.

In the area of ICTs, global feminist interventions already started well prior to WSIS, albeit in a manner that proved insufficient for the political scope of the Information Society as addressed in the course of WSIS. The most widely known feminist political precedent that offered a springboard to tackle ICTs further at WSIS was Section J "Women and the Media" of the Beijing Declaration and Platform for Action, agreed upon at the United Nations Fourth World Conference on Women in Beijing in 1995. Two strategic objectives regarding media and ICTs were codified then, one to "Increase the participation and access of women to expression and decision-making in and through the media and new technologies of communication" (UN 1995: strategic objective J.1) and the other to "Promote a balanced and non-stereotyped portrayal of women in the media" (UN 1995: strategic objective J.2).

ICTs at Beijing were largely addressed in their capacity as news and communication media, holding the potential to facilitate global feminist networking and knowledge dissemination about women's human rights. At the same time, strongly gender-stereotyped content had already become prevalent and was criticized at Beijing, as were the discriminatory employment structures of ICT-related businesses. Since all ICT concerns raised at Beijing have remained valid and unresolved, they were carried over into WSIS (see Jensen 2006).

After Beijing, further feminist interventions already addressed Information Society politics proper. Targeted and successful international gender advocacy in ICT policy was for instance carried out in 1998 at the World Telecommunications Development Conference organized by ITU in Valletta, Malta, in the wake of which ITU established a Gender Task Force (Hafkin 2002: 3). The subsequent WSIS process was then decisive because it constituted a unique focal point and further catalyst for the generation of knowledge about women's experiences and needs regarding media, ICTs and the multiple digital divides that have opened up. This knowledge was gathered and produced both inside and outside the UN system, and various stakeholders and entities fed it into the WSIS deliberations in the shape of political recommendations designed to promote gender equality, non-discrimination and women's empowerment. To give some examples from within the UN:

- The International Research and Training Institute for the Advancement of Women (INSTRAW) in 2002 held a Virtual Seminar Series on "Gender and ICTs" (see Huyer and Sikoska 2002).
- The Division for the Advancement of Women (DAW) held Expert Group Meetings the same year, one entitled "Information and Communication Technologies and their Impact on and Use as an Instrument for the Advancement and Empowerment of Women" (see UN DAW 2002a), and the other entitled "Participation and Access of Women to the Media, and the Impact of Media on and Its Use as an Instrument for the Advancement and Empowerment of Women" (see UN DAW 2002b).
- Taking into account the outcomes of the Expert Group Meetings, the Commission on the Status of Women (CSW) addressed "Participation and Access of Women to the Media, and Information and Communication Technologies and their Impact on and Use as an Instrument for the Advancement and Empowerment of Women" in its session of 2003 and submitted its conclusions to the WSIS process (see UN CSW 2003).
- The Inter-Agency Network on Women and Gender Equality (IANWGE) prepared and distributed briefing notes for WSIS on "Information and Communication Technology and Gender", covering the expertise of many different UN organizations.
- Two WSIS-related entities devoted to gender equality engaged in lobbying and advocacy during the entire first phase of the summit preparations, the WSIS Gender Caucus as a multi-stakeholder group and the NGO Gender Strategies Working Group as a civil society entity. Both entities merged in the WSIS Gender Caucus during the second WSIS phase and jointly continued their attempts to influence the political outcomes (see Jensen 2005).

The research brought together in contexts and groups such as the ones just named documented the following state of affairs as the basis for feminist advocacy: ICTs, left to market forces and governed by gender-blind policies, have tended to deepen existing social divides and to augment inequalities, including those between women and men. But many ICT projects and initiatives from around the world have demonstrated that the lives of girls and women can be bettered, and that social divides and injustices can be minimized or overcome, if ICTs are designed, implemented and monitored accordingly. However, to truly empower girls and women to become shapers of the Information Society and technologies, far reaching, structural changes are necessary. These changes have to counter the discrimination that many girls and women face with respect to different aspects of their lives, most notably in the following areas: formal and informal education, including the abilities to read and write one's native and other languages, media literacy, access to technologies, leisure time, opportunities to build a career, mobility, financial autonomy, emotional and practical support in one's endeavors, and validity accorded to one's world view, expertise and experiences.

One of the most prevalent approaches guiding the research to identify discrimination and inequalities faced by many groups of girls and women was the bottom-up approach, in which specific female constituencies and their needs or experiences were analyzed in order to stake claims on their behalf and make political recommendations (see Martínez and Reilly 2002, for an excellent example regarding e-governance in Latin America). Less often, a top-down approach was employed, which started from a scrutiny of policies or programs and assessed how they fell short of answering the needs of specific female constituencies (see Anand and Uppal 2002, addressing the management and regulation of ICTs).

Both approaches, bottom-up and top-down, can be understood as responses to at least two theoretical legacies that feminists have had to grapple with: One legacy is the obliteration of female constituencies and their concerns from the mainstream/malestream of research and politics, already referred to at the beginning of this section. Due to this legacy, political universalism has gone hand in hand with the unavailability of gender-disaggregated research data. The other legacy is the feminist realization that grounded research is needed to circumvent the pitfall of constructing a universalized female object. This object's abstraction would likely mask its white, middle-class particularity and dominant position vis-à-vis other groups of women who are subordinated on account of race, class and other factors.

The top-down approach to identify specific female constituencies and the impact of policies or programs on them can be seen as in partial agreement with the mandate of gender mainstreaming, which calls for a detailed analysis of how both gender groups would be impacted by a particular program or policy. To quote from the definition of gender mainstreaming arrived at by the UN Economic and Social Council:

> "It is a strategy for making women's as well as men's concerns and experiences an integral dimension of the design, implementation, monitoring and evaluation of policies and programmes in all political, economic and societal spheres so that women and men benefit equally and inequality is not perpetuated. The ultimate goal is to achieve gender equality." (UN ECOSOC 1997: paragraph I.A)

Prime omissions relating to gender mainstreaming up until today have been the analysis of groups of men, and, if men have been taken into account, the development of solutions that actually impact both gender groups in the direction of gender equality. Instead, even if groups of men have been analyzed, which has by and large not been the case in the WSIS-related research, what has usually been developed at the end are specific support measures for women and girls only, which do not solve the issue of how the male gender roles can be made to change correspondingly.

Two central methodologies have characterized the ways in which distinct groups of women have been made visible and claims on their behalf have been staked. These methodologies, the compensatory one and the critical one, are common throughout feminist politics and research, they are neither specific to ICTs nor to the WSIS process (compare Bonder 2002). The compensatory methodology focuses on the forms of discrimination that women have experienced in relation to their male peers and on ways of overcoming discrimination. This approach is very common in politics, and it can draw on a well-established canon of women's human rights, including those codified in the Convention on the Elimination of all Forms of Discrimination against Women (CEDAW) as the most comprehensive women's human rights instrument to date. For instance, when the digital divide between rural and urban areas in developing countries has been addressed as a gender issue, it has been explained that women make up the majority of the rural population. Women have hence borne the brunt of the infrastructural shortcomings of these areas, while men have tended to profit more from the superior infrastructure provided in cities. Consequently, political recommendations have focused on how to provide better infrastructure in rural areas and how to make it accessible for the women there.

The critical methodology emphasizes the unique perspectives and assets that women possess due to their traditional gender roles. It has been used to either simply valorize these perspectives and assets, or even to argue that these should be diffused more broadly. This strategy, it needs to be stressed, does not resonate so much with the sphere of politics but rather evokes the social sphere and cultural diversity. For instance, with the help of this methodology, it has been argued that software design by women follows specific patterns that arise from women's socialization and is hence valid and valuable as such. With a specific focus on women's roles as social mediators, it has further been argued that software design by women potentially takes more diverse users' needs into account than software designed by men who have been socialized to focus on their own perspectives alone. In this argument, software design by women would be superior to the prevalent male forms of software design.

Both methodologies, the compensatory and the critical one, often imply the masculine side of things as the norm or the status quo. They to a large extent leave intact the abstract quality of hegemonic masculinity, while women come to appear as a gendered and thus particularized interest group with specific concerns. While this is a clear shortcoming in academic terms, in political terms it may be somewhat effective insofar as demands based on this logic will potentially be taken up in political documents.

2   Feminist Achievements at WSIS and Their Limits

The most fundamental feminist battle at WSIS, which had to be fought for almost the entire four-year process, revolved around the recognition of the gender digital divide, and a reaffirmation of the principles of gender equality and women's empowerment as codified in Beijing in 1995. This struggle was finally successful, in that both the Geneva Declaration of Principles (UN 2003a) and the Tunis Commitment (UN 2005a) each contain a strong "women's paragraph". These read as follows:

"We affirm that development of ICTs provides enormous opportunities for women, who should be an integral part of, and key actors, in the Information Society. We are committed to ensuring that the Information Society enables women's empowerment and their full participation on the basis on [sic] equality in all spheres of society and in all decision-making processes. To this end, we should mainstream a gender equality perspective and use ICTs as a tool to that end." (UN 2003a: paragraph 12)

"We recognise that a gender divide exists as part of the digital divide in society and we reaffirm our commitment to women's empowerment and to a gender equality perspective, so that we can overcome this divide. We further acknowledge that the full participation of women in the Information Society is necessary to ensure the inclusiveness and respect for human rights within the Information Society. We encourage all stakeholders to support women's participation in decision-making processes and to contribute to shaping all spheres of the Information Society at international, regional and national levels." (UN 2005a: paragraph 23)

While these women's paragraphs clearly stipulate women's stakes and entitlements regarding ICTs and the Information Society, the paragraphs at the same time can be seen to connote the fact that women in the vast part of the documents are not again mentioned. As for the further gender-relevant provisions achieved at WSIS, three concurrent, prime rhetorical outcomes require attention: the rhetorical absence of men, the designation of women or girls as problem groups, and the equation of women and gender. The rhetorical absence of men means that in gender terms, the prevalent opposition is not between women and men but between women and the generic, abstract person. To quote paragraph 29 of the Geneva Declaration of Principles as an example:

"Each person should have the opportunity to acquire the necessary skills and knowledge in order to understand, participate actively in, and benefit fully from, the Information Society and the knowledge economy. Literacy and universal primary education are key factors for building a fully inclusive information society, paying particular attention to the special needs of girls and women." (UN 2003a: para. 29)

In keeping with this general rhetorical framework, and as a result of relentless feminist lobbying and advocacy, the WSIS documents contain a number of additional paragraphs that call for specific forms of affirmative action on behalf of girls and women. The Geneva Plan of Action (UN 2003b) refers to the participation of women in or through entrepreneurship, innovation and investment (para. C6.13.l), employment opportunities for women in telework (para. C7.19.c), women as health providers in the context of e-health (para. C7.18.e), and early intervention programs for young girls in science and technology to bring them into ICT careers (para. C.7.19.d). The Tunis Agenda (UN 2005b), while considerably less concerned with women, at least takes up ICT capacity building for women (para. 90.c) and ICT science and technology training and education to promote girls and women in decision-making regarding the Information Society (para. 90.d).

While calls for affirmative action – as discussed above regarding the compensatory feminist methodology – mostly arise from grounded research into girls' and women's roles and needs, their rhetoric suggests that women or girls are the problem groups. In other words, this strategy does not address groups of boys and men as those who are benefiting from unequal relationships or causing them. Instead, it seems to be presumed that girls and women will automatically become equal to their male peers if they are helped along. As already discussed, such a model does not take into account that gender is relational in terms of female and male roles, which both would need to change. Tellingly, the only paragraphs in all of the WSIS documents that explicitly mention men merely talk about the "inclusion of all men and women" (UN 2003b: para. D27) and "balanced and diverse portrayals of women and men by the media" (UN 2003b: para. C9.24.e).

The conceptual and political shortcoming just diagnosed can also be traced in that the terms "women" and "gender" often appear to be used interchangeably so that, as Greig, Kimmel and Lang stated in the quote reproduced above, gender comes to be understood as a women's issue. Thus the Geneva Plan of Action (UN 2003b) for instance slides from "removing the gender barriers to ICT education and training" to "promoting equal training opportunities in ICT-related fields for women and girls" (para. C4.11.g). Similarly, it moves from "gender-sensitive curricula in formal and non-formal education" to "enhancing communication and media literacy for women" (para. C8.23.h). Finally, it calls for "gender-specific indicators on ICT use and needs" in order to "assess the impact of funded ICT projects on the lives of women and girls" (para. E.28.d). In addition, there are two references to gender on its own, one addressing gender equality in the context of e-workers and e-employers (para. C7.19.a) and the other demanding gender analysis in the ICT Development (Digital Opportunity) Index (para. E.28.a).

Thus in essence, what we find is that gender concerns are largely presented as synonymous with special measures for women and girls, while boys and men remain the absent element in the gender equation. It has to be stressed yet again that an acknowledgment of girls and women and their needs, and a commitment to affirmative action on their behalf, is a clear victory of feminist lobbying and advocacy within WSIS. But such a political outcome faces severe limitations, which might effectively undermine the overall goals of gender equality and women's empowerment. So far, it has been argued that the logical corollary to the analysis that women appear as the marked and particularized gender is that men appear as unmarked by gender, and that this abstract position is the one of power in the gender hierarchy. Gender thus only manifests itself explicitly when girls or women are named – and hence stereotyped – as an interest group that needs specific forms of help. That this help can only have transformative potential when corresponding changes in the dominating gender group are triggered is completely beyond the pale within this ideology, because such a line of thought would particularize the dominant gender group and draw attention to the fact that it subordinates the other gender group.

Equally decisive for the perpetuation of hegemonic masculinity is the fact that women's and girls' concerns invariably appear as marginal add-ons beyond the central agenda and issues tackled in a given political process. This state of affairs reflects the fact that the political agenda of core issues generally remains immune to feminist interventions. Hegemonic masculinity thus not only thrives through the omission of representing a particularized male gender, but the resulting universalism is substantiated by a plethora of concepts and issues that ultimately privilege powerful men and specific notions of masculinity.

To clarify this argument, it is instructive to briefly turn to film theorist Dyer and his analysis of how positions of dominance are represented but come to appear as unmarked. Dyer (1997) has elaborated these mechanisms with respect to the racial category of whiteness, tied to the gender category of masculinity. According to him, whiteness in general and white masculinity in particular has reserved for itself a "position of being without properties, unmarked, universal, just human" (p. 38) from which it can observe and dominate those it has marked as "other". To be sure, white people, and most certainly white men, are at the center of western representational regimes. So their claim to universality is indeed transported through representation, but in a very particular way. To quote Dyer:

> "There is a specificity to white representation, but it does not reside in a set of stereotypes so much as in **narrative structural positions, rhetorical tropes** and **habits of perception** [my emphasis]. The same is true of all representation – the taxonomic study of stereotypes was only ever an initial step in the study of non-white representation. However, stereotyping – complex and contradictory though it is [...] – does characterize the representation of subordinated social groups and is one of the means by which they are categorized and kept in their place, whereas white people in white culture are given the illusion of their own infinite variety." (Dyer 1997: 12)

Thus at issue are two representational contexts or levels, the one of stereotypes, which appears more prevalent with regard to the dominated social position, and the one of narrative positions, tropes and ingrained ways of perceiving things, which seems to be more relevant for perpetuating positions of dominance. With this qualification in mind, it can be stipulated that negotiations which perpetuate hegemonic masculinity are not explicitly about specific groups of men and their goals, preferences or needs, but they are about supposedly gender-neutral concepts or issues, and these issues add up to an agenda. Correspondingly, on the broad plane of politics in general and in International Relations (IR) in particular, feminist critics have argued early on that core concepts, from citizenship, autonomy and sovereignty, to diplomacy, conflict and war, have been defined on male terms and as male terms, rooted in the gender hierarchy and the suppression of the supposedly inferior, female aspects, traits or positions (see e.g. Lister 1997). Rendering "the hidden masculine gender of IR theory and practice visible" (True 1996: 213) was an important step towards preparing the intellectual ground for understanding how current political agendas may bolster hegemonic masculinity.

3   The Universalized Male WSIS Agenda

At the outset, it needs to be stated that international politics is of course not only a field in which male predominance is perpetuated as a unified force, but also a field in which widely diverging political interests clash. Thus it can be claimed that in international politics, the position of non-marked, non-gendered universality is extended from white men to those non-white men – and the few women who have entered this arena – who succeed in framing issues and getting them on the political agenda. The agenda of issues is hence the outcome of power struggles largely among privileged men. As for WSIS, this summit was initially planned by ITU with a largely technological focus, and its conceptualization coincided with the boom of ICTs, the internet and the new market, which created an economic euphoria in the global north. When the negotiations started in earnest, the development perspective became more contoured, with attention to the digital divide, the Millennium Development Goals (MDGs) and ICT for Development (ICT4D). Central political contestations, not surprisingly, revolved around power and money, but ultimately did not successfully challenge the prevailing forces:

- The issue of Internet Governance contested the Internet Corporation for Assigned Names and Numbers (ICANN) and the USA.
- The issue of financing mechanisms to bridge the digital divide contested models of development cooperation including funds and public-private partnerships, and it ultimately contested the prevailing neo-liberal policy approach to markets and economies.
- Human rights issues, most importantly freedom of expression, communication rights and the right to privacy versus national security, contested autonomy and sovereignty at the individual, corporate, and national levels.
- Issues of media diversity, media concentration control, and the status of community media contested media monopolies and national media regulation.
- The issues of intellectual property rights versus knowledge commons and public resources, and of proprietary software versus free and open source software, contested existing copyright, patent and trademark regimes.

Of these issues, the first two proved to be so controversial that they dominated the political WSIS process of the entire second phase up until Tunis. None of the issues was treated in a manner that involved an explicit mentioning of the gendered constituencies and their various stakes in it. True to the conceptual history of politics, the discussion only implied abstract entities such as national governments, citizens and private enterprises. Now why, given that feminists surely have been very interested in contesting money flows and power as well, was it not possible to engender the issues and the agenda, to mainstream the gender perspective into the negotiations more broadly?

To answer this question, it is vital to consider the processes of agenda setting in more detail. Since the agenda was not identified with groups of women and men and their relationships in mind, it by default did not give center stage to concerns that have been most pressing from a feminist or gender equality point of view. For instance, according to the worldwide evaluation undertaken for the 10th anniversary of the Beijing Declaration and Platform for Action in 2005, the structurally subordinate position of girls and women has been cemented all over the world by threats and actual acts of violence directed at them, by a disproportionate amount of unpaid reproductive and care work that has been relegated to them and by the poverty that many women have experienced, for instance as a result of their discriminatory employment and social security situations (see UN Office of the Secretary-General 2004). Quite obviously, such issues would never have made it onto the political agenda of a UN World Summit on the Information Society, even though they are of course highly pertinent to the formulation of any utopia, including that of the Information Society.

Another example, this time from within the WSIS agenda, is the issue of free and open source software (FOSS) versus proprietary software. This was one of the "hot" issues: For the global north, the monetary stakes are high because of the revenues generated by licensing proprietary software. For the global south, the development stakes are high, both in terms of employing FOSS to build the capacity to write software and in terms of the possibility to avoid licensing fees for proprietary software to the north. How is this issue gendered? Those who make the bulk of the money from proprietary software in the north are male, most notably CEOs and boards of directors of transnational corporations as well as owners of businesses or company shares. Yet those who develop FOSS are largely male, too, this picture does not change substantially with the kind of software created and the business model applied. All other things being equal, those who are most likely to become new writers of FOSS will also be male.

To illustrate the many steps by which the majority of girls and women are removed from this issue – and here the compensatory methodology is employed and reference is made to the women's and girls' issues mentioned in the second section of this article – suffice it to point out that girls and women would need the same kind of education as boys, the same access to and confidence in handling technologies, the same amount of free time and pocket money to experiment with technology, the same peer group support within the open source community and so on and so forth. Simultaneously, men would have to give up their homosocial hold on the communities and businesses concerned with software writing, and they would have to relinquish the gender stereotype of the male software writer/genius who either builds an evil empire or is a Robin-Hood-like FOSS hero. Men would have to step back and enable women financially, time-wise and emotionally to dedicate working time or spare time to the task of writing software. All of this is not to say that many feminists do not champion FOSS. It is just to illustrate the many additional layers that appear when a gender perspective is applied to specify the obstacles encountered by the majority of girls and women in such a context. This explains why political issues of that kind might not be uppermost on a feminist agenda.

At the same time, it needs to be pointed out that a bottom-up approach, particularly one that restricts itself to a focus on the most disadvantaged groups, is unlikely to allow girls and women ever to catch up in time to arrive on the global political scene for real power-brokering. To stay with the example of FOSS: Power at WSIS was brokered through a rhetoric that suggests that different software models could simultaneously be promoted and coexist peacefully, while evidence is accumulating that intellectual property rights with regard to software might increasingly be applied and abused to hinder FOSS development. Meanwhile, as was laid out in the previous paragraph, concrete girls' and women's issues were stipulated at the bottom level of education in general and ICT education in particular, but remained essentially unrelated to specific software models and intellectual property rights.

A similar case about the need for feminists to impact the highest levels of power brokering can be made regarding the issue of Internet Governance, which was a defining issue of the second WSIS phase. While the Tunis Commitment, as quoted, reaffirms the necessity to bring women into decision-making processes, Internet Governance as a prime decision-making arena for the Information Society framed in the Tunis Agenda is devoid of references to women's participation. In this context, the feminist lobbying and advocacy that called for a fifty-fifty gender balance in Internet Governance remained unheeded. At the same time, it needs to be conceded that no agreement could be reached among feminists at WSIS about what exactly Internet Governance should encompass and which stakeholders should principally engage in it. But Internet Governance is such a new field that agreement about these issues hardly exists anywhere, so that even a general, tentative definition of the issue itself was only developed and agreed upon within the overall WSIS process shortly before the Tunis summit.

And as argued by Banks, Doria and Morris (2005), it is vital for feminists to engage with global political processes such as these right from the start in order to be able to contribute to the definition of the new structures and institutions that are being built and the issues that get tackled in them. If this does not happen, hegemonic masculinity by default will successfully perpetuate itself in these structures and institutions, not least through the demarcation and definition of issues and agendas. To try and rectify such a default setup later on, for instance with the help of gender mainstreaming, poses the risk that this strategy may be employed within an overall framework or with regard to an agenda of issues that can be far removed from, unrelated to or at worst detrimental to the aims of gender equality and women's empowerment.

4   Conclusion

The UN World Summit on the Information Society of 2003 and 2005 attests to the fact that ICTs and the Internet have become globally recognized as a new field of political and economic power brokering, since these technologies have begun to deeply restructure the world. Feminists rose to the challenge of influencing the WSIS political process in the direction of gender equality, non-discrimination and women's empowerment. They have achieved a twofold gain regarding the outcome documents. At the level of principles, they have gained recognition and an overall commitment to their goals, which are now expressed in two strong "women's paragraphs". At the level of concrete actions, they have achieved a number of commitments to affirmative action on behalf of girls and women, most notably regarding education, training, work and career choices. This outcome, however, while incredibly hard-won, does not go much beyond what was agreed upon globally at the Fourth World Conference on Women in Beijing over a decade ago.

When analyzed from a Gender Studies perspective, the underlying mechanisms that favor political results like these become clear, suggesting that power has not been successfully challenged in such a scenario: By gaining a combination of sweeping political promises to women and a few bottom-up initiatives for women and girls, the female half of the population comes to appear as a marginal, stereotyped interest group whose problems can be addressed by apocryphal affirmative action directed at them. Meanwhile, hegemonic masculinity perpetuates itself without drawing attention to itself as gendered, and by extension without drawing attention to patriarchy as such.

Thus male privilege is not considered as something that needs to be eradicated through concrete actions and strategies laid out in the WSIS documents.

It is also not considered as something that leads to a specific worldview and identification of issues that are unlikely to be in keeping with the issues that appear most pressing from the vantage points and positions of the dominated groups. Hegemonic male dominance remains inscribed in the very choice of issues and agendas for a political process such as WSIS, and it further reconsolidates itself successfully in the bargaining process and its outcomes. Feminists have not been able to impact the larger political agenda or to insert gender considerations into the core issues of power brokering at WSIS, from Internet Governance to financial mechanisms to bridge the digital divide, and from copyright, patent and trademark regimes to national security.

Given the intricate ways gender works in concrete and abstract ways as well as avowed and disavowed forms, there is an urgent need for feminists to employ multiple tactics at different levels. With regard to the grassroots level, they have to continue promoting bottom-up initiatives such as girls' and women's computer literacy programs. But also at this level, boys and men need to be "engendered" and educated to develop peaceful and cooperative forms of masculinity for themselves. This means that they need to be taught to reject hegemonic masculinity and patriarchal dividends. Beyond the grassroots level, the fight for women's equal participation in top-level decision making arenas needs to continue, with special attention to arenas that are being newly created, as for instance the Internet Governance Forum inaugurated in the wake of WSIS. In these arenas, a complex engendering of power issues and an understanding of who argues over them and with what motives is required to expose hegemonic masculine interests and dynamics that consolidate patriarchal setups. These tasks require concerted feminist efforts to analyze and challenge agendas, issues and their framing; it is not sufficient for feminists to gain access and voting rights. On this basis, new alliances need to be sought that challenge hegemonic masculinity.

Regarding the WSIS implementation and follow-up process, the WSIS commitment to gender equality and women's empowerment as a characteristic of the Information Society can be considered a useful entry point for further feminist interventions. Given the high likelihood of a continuation of far-reaching ICT-induced changes, the ferment and upheaval linked with these developments will persistently open hegemonic positions to challenge and will thus favor ongoing feminist contestations. These opportunities need to be seized at all levels.

References

Anand, Anita; Uppal, Mahesh (2002): Engendering Management and Regulation of ICTs: Narrowing the Digital Divide for Women. Background paper for UN INSTRAW Virtual Seminar Series on Gender and ICTs, Seminar Three: En-gendering Management and Regulation of ICTs (29 July to 9 August 2002). Available at: http://www.uninstraw.org/en/docs/gender_and_ict/Annand.pdf (last accessed: 18 February 2006)

Banks, Karen; Doria, Avri; Morris, Jacqueline (2005): The Working Group on Internet Governance: A Feminist Conversation. In: Drossou, Olga; Jensen, Heike (eds.): Visions in Process II: The World Summit on the Information Society Geneva 2003-Tunis 2005. Berlin: Heinrich-Böll-Stiftung: 62-68. Available at: http://www.world summit2003.de/download_en/Visions-in-Process-II.pdf (last accessed: 18 February 2006)

Bonder, Gloria (2002): From Access to Appropriation: Women and ICT policies in Latin American [sic] and the Caribbean. UN DAW Expert Group Meetings on Information and Communication Technologies and their Impact on and Use as an Instrument for the Advancement and Empowerment of Women. Seoul, Republic of Korea, 11 to 14 November 2002 (document EGM/ICT/2002/EP.3, dated 29 November 2002). Available at: http://www.un.org/womenwatch/daw/egm/ict2002/reports/Paper-GBonder. PDF (last access: 18 February 2006)

Connell, Robert W. (1995): Masculinities. Berkeley, Los Angeles: University of California Press.

Dyer, Richard (1997): White. London, New York: Routledge.

Greig, Alan; Kimmel, Michael; Lang, James (2000): Men, Masculinities and Development: Broadening our work towards gender equality. Gender in Development Monograph Series #10, May 2000. New York: UNDP.

Hafkin, Nancy (2002): Gender Issues in ICT Policy in Developing Countries: An Overview. UN DAW Expert Group Meeting on Information and Communication Technologies and their Impact on and Use as an Instrument for the Advancement and Empowerment of Women. Seoul, Republic of Korea, 11 to 14 November 2002 (document EGM/ICT/2002/EP.1, dated 25 October 2002). Available at: http://www.un. org/womenwatch/daw/egm/ict2002/reports/Paper-NHafkin.PDF (last accessed: 18 February 2006)

Huyer, Sofia; Sikoska, Tatjana (2002): Instraw Virtual Seminar Series on Gender and Information and Communication Technologies (ICTs): Summary of Discussions and Recommendations. UN DAW Expert Group Meeting on Information and Communication Technologies and their Impact on and Use as an Instrument for the Advancement and Empowerment of Women. Seoul, Republic of Korea, 11 to 14 November 2002 (document EGM/ICT/2002/OP.3, dated 6 November 2002). Available at: http://www.un.org/womenwatch/daw/egm/ict2002/reports/Paper%20by%20INSTR AW.PDF (last accessed: 18 February 2006)

Jensen, Heike (2006, in print): Women, Media and ICTs in UN Politics: Progress or Backlash? In: IT for Change, APDIP (ed.): Gender in the Information Society: Emerging Issues. Bangkok: UNDP-APDIP.

Jensen, Heike (2005): Gender Equality and the Multi-Stakeholder Approach: WSIS as Best Practice? In: Drossou, Olga; Jensen, Heike (eds.): Visions in Process II: The World Summit on the Information Society Geneva 2003-Tunis 2005. Berlin: Heinrich-Böll-Stiftung: 53-61. Available at: http://www.worldsummit2003.de/ download_en/Visions-in-Process-II.pdf (last accessed: 18 February 2006)

Lister, Ruth (1997): Citizenship: Feminist Perspectives. Houndmills, Basingstoke, Hampshire, London: Macmillan.

Martínez, Juliana; Reilly, Katherine (2002): Looking Behind the Internet: Empowering Women for Public Policy Advocacy in Central America. UN INSTRAW Virtual Seminar Series on Gender and ICTs, Seminar Four: ICTs as Tools for Bridging the Gender Digital Divide and Women's Empowerment (2-14 September 2002). Available at: http://www.un-instraw.org/en/docs/gender_and_ict/Martinez.pdf (last accessed: 18 February 2006)

True, Jacqui (1996): Feminism. In: Scott Burchill; Linklater, Andrew (eds.): Theories of International Relations. New York: St. Martin's: 210-251.

United Nations (1995): Beijing Declaration and Platform for Action adopted by the Fourth World Conference on Women on 15 September 1995 (document A/CONF.177/20/Rev.1 (96.IV.13)). Available at: http://www.un.org/womenwatch/ daw/beijing/platform/ (last accessed: 19 February 2006)

United Nations (2003a): Declaration of Principles adopted by the World Summit on the Information Society on 12 December 2003 (document WSIS-03/GENEVA/DOC/4-E). Available at: http://www.itu.int/dms_pub/itu-s/md/03/wsis/doc/S03-WSIS-DOC-0004!!PDF-E.pdf (last accessed: 19 February 2006)

United Nations (2003b): Plan of Action adopted by the World Summit on the Information Society on 12 December 2003 (document WSIS-03/GENEVA/DOC/5-E). Available at: http://www.itu.int/dms_pub/itu-s/md/03/wsis/doc/S03-WSIS-DOC-0005!!PDF-E.pdf (last accessed: 19 February 2006)

United Nations (2005a): Tunis Commitment adopted by the World Summit on the Information Society on 18 November 2005 (document WSIS-05/TUNIS/DOC/7-E). Available at: http://www.itu.int/wsis/docs2/tunis/off/7.pdf (last accessed: 19 February 2006)

United Nations (2005b): Tunis Agenda for the Information Society adopted by the World Summit on the Information Society on 18 November 2005 (document WSIS-05/TUNIS/DOC/6(Rev.1)-E). Available at: http://www.itu.int/wsis/docs2/tunis/off/ 6rev1.pdf (last accessed: 19 February 2006)

United Nations Commission on the Status of Women (UN CSW) (2003): Participation and Access of Women to the Media, and Information and Communication Technologies and their Impact on and Use as an Instrument for the Advancement and Empowerment of Women: Agreed Conclusions. New York, USA, 14 March 2003 (Forty-seventh Session, 3-14 March 2003). Available at: http://www.un.org/women watch/daw/csw/csw47/AC-mediaICT-auv.PDF (last accessed: 18 February 2006)

United Nations Division for the Advancement of Women (UN DAW) (2002a): Information and Communication Technologies and their Impact on and Use as an Instrument
for the Advancement and Empowerment of Women: Report of the Expert Group
Meeting Seoul, Republic of Korea, 11-14 November 2002 (document EGM/ICT/
2002/Report, dated 23 December 2002). Available at: http://www.un.org/women
watch/daw/egm/ict2002/reports/EGMFinalReport.pdf (last accessed: 18 February
2006)
United Nations Division for the Advancement of Women (UN DAW) (2002b): Participation and Access of Women to the Media, and the Impact of Media on and Its Use as
an Instrument for the Advancement and Empowerment of Women: Report of the
Expert Group Meeting Beirut, Lebanon, 12-15 November 2002 (document
EGM/MEDIA/2002/Report). Available at: http://www.un.org/womenwatch/daw/
egm/media2002/reports/EGMFinalReport.PDF (last accessed: 18 February 2006)
United Nations Economic and Social Council (UN ECOSOC) (1997): Gender Mainstreaming. Agreed Conclusions 1997/2 adopted on 18 September 1997. Available at: http://
www.un.org/womenwatch/daw/csw/GMS.PDF (last accessed: 19 February 2006)
United Nations Office of the Secretary-General (2004): Review of the Implementation of
the Beijing Platform for Action and the Outcome Documents of the Special Session
of the General Assembly entitled Women 2000: Gender Equality, Development and
Peace for the Twenty-first Century - Report of the Secretary-General (document
E/CN.6/2005/2, dated 6 December 2004). Available at: http://daccessdds.un.org/doc/
UNDOC/GEN/N04/636/83/PDF/N0463683.pdf?OpenElement (last accessed: 18
February 2006)

II Analysis and Deconstruction

'Social' Robots & 'Emotional' Software Agents: Gendering Processes and De-Gendering Strategies for 'Technologies in the Making'[8]

Jutta Weber, Corinna Bath

Introduction

Over the past years we can observe profound reconfigurations of the boundaries between human beings and machines in the field of artificial intelligence (AI) and computer science. Particularly software agents and robots attest to an ongoing paradigm shift from machine-oriented concepts, algorithms and automats towards 'interaction' (see Wegner 1997, Crutzen 2003). While early approaches sought to model rational-cognitive processes and to solve problems using formal structures, the emphasis is currently shifting to human-computer and human-robot interaction.

Recently artifacts such as software agents and robots are often conceptualized as friendly, understanding and believable partners which communicate 'naturally' with users and support them in everyday life. 'Sociable', humanoid robots are designed to take care of old or sick people. Software agents are expected to obtain information independently. In order to serve users and give them advice, they appear human-like on the screen.

In this paper we examine the recent trend in AI to build 'social' and 'emotional' artifacts from a feminist technology studies perspective. Starting from prominent visions of socio-emotional machines, some prototypes and commercial products, which currently came into use, we point out gendering aspects in their representation and the underlying concepts. Focusing on societal preconditions of socially intelligent machines, we will ask how traditional feminist critiques of technology might apply to these new artifacts. The arguments will lead us to point out some basic problems of developing de-gendering strategies

---

8 This chapter is a revised version of our paper published in: Archibald, Jacqueline; Emms, Judy; Grundy, Frances; Payne, Janet; Turner, Eva (eds.): The Gender Politics of ICT. Middlesex University Press 2005. It was presented at the Women Into Computing Conference, London 2005.

for 'technologies in the making'.[9] We finally propose dimensions and strategies for a contemporary feminist critique of technology.

1   The Vision of Sociable or Socially Intelligent Robots and Software Agents

Cynthia Breazeal from the Massachusetts Institute of Technology (MIT) is one of the leading researchers in the field of social robotics. Her vision of a sociable robot is a good example that clarifies the robot researchers' promises:

> "For me, a sociable robot is able to communicate and interact with us, understand and even relate to us, in a personal way. It should be able to understand us and itself in social terms. We, in turn, should be able to understand it in the same social terms - to be able to relate to it and to empathize with it. Such a robot must be able to a-dapt and learn throughout its lifetime, incorporating shared experiences with other individuals into its understanding of self, of others, and of the relationships they sha-re. In short, a sociable robot is socially intelligent in a human-like way, and interac-ting with it is like interacting with another person. At the pinnacle of achievement, they could befriend us, as we could them." (Breazeal 2002: 1)

She stresses that social artifacts that become part of our daily life must be able to adapt to users in a natural and intuitive manner – not vice versa. Her 'master-piece' – as she calls it – the robotic creature Kismet is designed to interact physically, affectively and socially with humans, in order to learn from them. The man-machine-relation (or should one say the woman-machine-relation?) is modeled according to that of a caregiver and a human infant. We found similar attempts in software agent research. Researchers stress that they aim at building *"emotional relationships by long-term interactions wherein the two parties pay attention to the emotional state of the other, communicate their feelings, share a trust, feel empathetic, and establish a connection, a bond."* (Stern 2002: 336). In some commercial computer games like 'Virtual Petz' or 'Virtual Babyz' the characters try to seek the users' attention in order to interact with them, to get 'care' and to get 'socialized' by the users.

---

9   The idea of 'technologies in the making' refers to contemporary approaches to the social studies of science and technology (e.g. Latour 1987). Instead of considering technologies as 'ready-made' or analyzing their context of use, we aim to track the development of technologies in a constantly shifting, multifaceted network of artifacts, disciplinary foundations, scientific methods, social preconditions and cultural meanings within a transdisciplinary and controversial universe of discourse.

To realize these envisioned social behaviors of machines researchers utilize models and theories from the fields of psychology, cognitive science, and ethnology, thereby aiming at the computation of social and emotional competencies.

2 Anthropomorphism and Gendering

If we take a look at the first prototypes and commercial products that were intended to be social we have to admit that they do not appear very innovative, at least with regard to the predominant gender concepts - if not to say stereotypes – used. Cyberella, a presentation agent created at the German Research Center for Artificial Intelligence (http://www.dfki.de/cyberella), and the robot "Valerie, a domestic android" (http://www.androidworld.com/prod19.htm) for instance, were given a kind of super feminine shape.

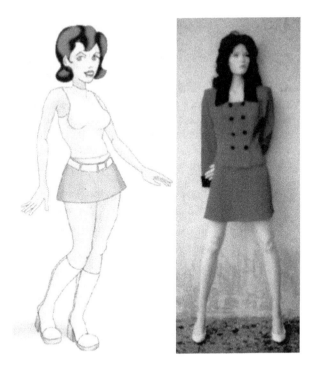

Figure 1: Cyberella and Valerie

Other software agents chat with users in a strongly gender stereotyped or even sexualized manner. Even though some of the new social artifacts appear more 'neutral' or less gender-stereotyped at a first glance they are nevertheless modeled on the ground of questionable ontological presumptions. The way how Cynthia Breazeal's interaction with Kismet is represented, for example, reshapes the wo/man-machine relationship into a gendered caregiver-infant relationship.

The visions and realizations of social artifacts in software agent research and robotics raise many questions:

What and whose understanding of sociality and emotionality is underlying these new artifacts? Is it desirable from a critical, feminist perspective to develop 'emotional' artifacts we are supposed to empathize with? Do artifacts modeled in terms of caregiver-infant-relationships represent a critical understanding of social behavior?

Or, more general: Is it desirable and promising to model human-machine-relationships according to those among humans? Are artifacts like Valerie and Cyberella based on anthropological and ontological premises concerning human behavior, relationships and emotions that we can agree to from a critical, feminist perspective?

In order to judge these developments of 'social' artifacts, we have to take seriously today's researchers' dream of a new and potent generation of socially intelligent artifacts. The implementation of sociality and emotionality into artifacts has become a center of attention in numerous research & development projects in the field of robotics and software agents. Recently, research laboratories emerge at several respectable universities labelled 'affective computing'. Some web sites, e-commerce or electronic tutor systems and computer games are already populated with software agents that are said to be endowed with a rudimentary personality and express simple forms of emotions. Moreover, robots are intended to become socialized and educated by their interaction with humans.

We now want to reflect these developments in the light of feminist critiques of technology.

3   Feminist Critique of Technology: Against Abstraction

During the last decades feminist scholars as well as other critics pointed out the lack of embodiment and situatedness in AI research (see e.g. Dreyfus 1963; Becker 1992). They stressed that researchers did not take into account the context and the social dimension of technology. The limited orientation towards rational-cognitive models and symbol processing was questioned. The critique often focused on the reductionist modeling of thought, on the simple understanding of human planning and acting as a merely rational-cognitive process and on approaches to problem solving constrained by the use of formal structures (see e.g. Suchman 1987).[10]

While much of the argumentation aimed against abstraction, disembodyment, decontextualization and the lack of the social dimension, it seems as if these critiques were now recognized by emergent technosciences. Meanwhile technology designers incorporate certain concepts of embodiment and situatedness into intelligent artifacts. While embodied robotics (see Pfeifer and Scheier 1999) and situated intelligent software agents are displacing symbol-oriented approaches in AI[11] we are now faced with the vision of ,social machines'. Researchers aim at developing machines beyond the limits of rational-cognitive grounded intelligence. They discover social behavior as the basis of 'real' intelligence. How can the shift from rational to social behavior be perceived from a critical point of view? Will chances for feminist intervention arise along these changes or will the envisioned dissolution of the dichotomy of human beings and machines cement the existing gender order?

The illustrations of robots and software agents we gave in the introduction of this paper already referred to our sceptical stance towards the 'innovative' potential of these so-called social machines. We ask: Why are the promised helpful, believable and trustworthy artifacts modeled according to crude gender stereotypes? Why is the mother-child relationship assumed to be a good model for the human-machine-relationship? And what should we think of the concept of social intelligence, which is now becoming popular in technoscientific discourses and practices?[12]

There is another point that makes us feel uncomfortable: Sociality and emotionality have been deeply gendered categories in western thought. These characteristics have traditionally been assigned to the feminine realm. And it is not by chance that we find a relatively large number of women developing social robots and software agents compared to other areas of old-fashioned, symbol-oriented AI or biomimetic robotics. It appears as if their so-called ,natural' competencies of sociality, communication etc. predetermined them to work in such a field. What could be more attractive than a nice-looking woman such as Cynthia Breazeal who embodies a true loving caregiver for a helpless infant robotic creature that needs training and caring to develop intelligence, social behavior, emotions and a personality?

---

10   See (Adam 1998) for an overview on feminist critique of AI.
11   For a discussion of philosophical and feminist influences on AI see for example (Sengers 1999).
12   The concept of social intelligence was developed at least partly because of the feminist critique of androcentric conceptions of evolution; see (Fausto-Sterling 1985; Hubbard 1979).

We approach the question of how to interpret recent developments in technology design by Bettina Heintz' critical approach to AI. In her paper *"Papiermaschinen. Die sozialen Voraussetzungen maschineller Intelligenz"*[13] the feminist science studies scholar and sociologist pointed towards the social and societal preconditions and implications of the mechanization of thought and everyday life with AI. On the one hand she claimed that first of all it were human beings who adapted themselves to the machine. Otherwise our unimaginative machines would not work at all. For example, secretaries are instructed to use a very simple language avoiding any ambiguities in order to enable software programs to translate their texts into another language. Thus the abilities we regard as genuine ones of computers are often the result of our own efficient work. And often we unconsciously compensate for the deficiencies of the machines, while at the same time our readiness to perceive machines as intelligent stems from our tendency to interpret our reality as loaded or even structured with meaning (see also Collins 1990). Following these arguments, the critique should not challenge primarily the claim that computers might become intelligent, but has to question the conditions that make us believe in the intelligence of machines.

On the other hand Bettina Heintz pointed out that a kind of mechanization of everyday life must have already taken place before the computer entered this process. The translation of problems into algorithms only becomes possible when humans already act in a rule-oriented way. A standardization of human behavior is necessary to model and develop software applications. What is the background in our society that elicits rule-oriented behavior that can be found so frequently?

Having feminist critiques in mind, we ask: what does it mean that techno-scientists anthropomorphize machines and discover sociality and emotionality as the cure for our still unimaginative, rational-cognitive grounded machines.[14] It seems that traditional strategies of wo/man-machine-communication are turned upside-down. While for a long time humans had to behave rationally and rule-oriented to make symbol-oriented machines successful, now machines are to become social in order to increase their usability and make them more helpful for human users. It is the machine now which is supposed to mimic or even learn those abilities and characteristics which were until recently regarded as purely and typically human and beyond the grasp of machines.

---

13   'Paper machines. The Social (Pre-)Conditions of Machine Intelligence'.
14   While roboticists and software agent researchers often point towards the tendency of anthropomorphization in the human-robot or human-computer interaction (Duffy 2003; Fong, Nourbakhsh, Dautenhahn 2003.; Gratch et. al 2002; Cassell et al. 2000), they rarely reflect on the additional work of humans to make sense of machinic behavior (see e.g. Suchman (in prep.) on the relationship between Breazeal and Kismet).

Rethinking Heintz' argument in the light of socially intelligent machines does not mean to ask whether and how machines can be or become social, but what makes us think of machines as social. What concepts of sociality and emotionality are predominant in today's AI and why? And what are the societal conditions under which machines are perceived as social and emotional?

Every socially intelligent machine we can dream of is still based on rule-oriented behavior, since this is the material ground and fundamental functionality of these machines. Therefore it is rule-oriented social behavior that is at the core of the theoretical approaches, concepts and practices of software agent researchers and roboticists. The kind of rules might differ in diverse strands of AI, but a standardization of human behavior is a precondition for every computer model and software application. Anthropomorphized machines are intended to operate by simulating social *norms*, supposed gender differences and other *stereotypes*. The starting point of these prototypes and implementations is rule-based social behavior that is said to be performed by humans. Researchers often use folk psychological and sociological approaches to sociality and emotionality in modeling human-machine-relations. Out of the wide range of psychology and sociology they particularly chose those theories for the computational modeling that assume that social behavior is operational.

And it is not by accident that software agent research and social robotics are working with sociological and socio-psychological approaches that explicitly use gender dichotomies and stereotypes. For example, we could detect a case which utilizes a feminist approach to improve human interaction with social machines: The computer scientist Daniel Moldt and the sociologist Christian von Scheve (2002) point out the value of roles, class and sex/gender differences in social interaction and their usefulness to minimize the contingency and to maximize the prediction of the behavior of the alter ego – of the human or machine partner in social interactive processes. Generally, in the realm of human-computer interaction emotions are considered to be useful to influence users, to convey intentionality and to smooth interactions. Referring to feminist sociologist Arlie Hochschild Moldt and von Scheve claim that emotions are based on a system of values and norms. Interrelations between emotions and social norms play a crucial role in matching the expectations of the alter ego. Moldt and von Scheve regard roles, class, gender and other differences as ideal categories in order to determine this relationship. Inspired by these ideas they strive for software agents that express emotions based on prevailing systems of values and norms. They assume that on this basis software agents appear intelligent, social and endowed with a personality (see Moldt and von Scheve 2002).

Not all of these new approaches, which aim to implement sociality into machines, exploit critical theories and feminist approaches in such a way. Nevertheless, this example shows that the paradigm shift from rational-cognitive to social machines does not lead to a de-gendering of technology design. The approach considered rather points to the fact that gender stereotypes are instrumentalized in order to build ‚better‘ machines that are perceived as socially intelligent.

Obviously, recent research in the field of software agents and social robotics is not primarily about making machines social as most researchers suggest. Rather it seems to be about training humans in rule-oriented social behavior. Only by relying on the latter the interaction with these machines can be made intelligible: As much as secretaries have to use an impoverished language to be able to use computer translation software, it will be necessary to use impoverished ways of interacting to respond to these social robots and artifacts. And while researchers use social norms and stereotypes to make their artifacts more consistent, convincing and believable, training humans in stereotypical behavior supports ways of acting which are predictable and therefore more exploitable in economic terms.

4   De-gendering Technologies: Dimensions and Strategies of Critique

Regarding recent developments in software agent research and social robotics it becomes obvious that we need a broader and highly differentiated feminist critique of artifacts and processes in AI and computer science. In the following we want to sharpen our analysis of de-gendering technologies with the insights given so far. Our intention is neither to develop a step-by-step recipe for necessary feminist interventions into technology design nor to give an overview of possible political practices, but to rethink strategies, tools and dimensions of feminist technoscience studies in the light of recent developments in the field of socially inspired AI and computer science.

4.1 Gender Representation

Rethinking sexist images or strongly gender stereotyped speech patterns used in social robotics and software agent research, obviously requires a critique of these stereotypes, patterns, norms and roles. This kind of critique of technology design targeting at *gendered representation* is well-established in feminist media studies. Often it is even shared by some (male) computer scientists. But what we wanted to point out here is that it is not sufficient only to revise the design of technology in the sense of wiping out its explicit or implicit gender stereotypes.

Nor would it be satisfying even to eliminate these and other social norms, roles and stereotypes like those of class, of age, of race, of sexuality etc. Gendered ontological and epistemological claims are also encoded in theoretical concepts that form the base for technological construction and software applications, such as the changing understanding of the social and the conceptualization of the human-machine relationship.

4.2 Social Theory

The relation between 'social machines' and the standardization of everyday life should be explored from a *social theory* perspective. It is the question whether we live in a society where social relations in general or at least in specific realms are already enacted in terms of rule-oriented behavior. Think for example of the standardization of health care for elderly people where every little service – like e.g. combing the hair, washing the back, etc. – is measured by standardized time schedules (minutes) and prices. In these realms the idea of social robots taking care of elderly people lies at hand. At the same time the standardization of social behavior through agents and robots might also lead to more rule-oriented behavior.

Another relevant aspect is linked to the question whether social machines are expected to fill in personal and relational vacancies that emerge with new social and work requirements in the age of globalisation. Will personal agents and robots that empathize with us and to whom we are befriended be a substitute for personal human relations in the age of mobility and change? Which deficiencies of our social life in the neo-liberal economy are supposed to be ‚repaired‘ by those artifacts?

4.3 Anthropological and Ontological Dimensions

From a critical perspective questions of anthropological and ontological assumptions arise on which technoscientific concepts in the fields of AI and software agent research are built. What is the underlying understanding of society, sociality and human interaction? How is the relation of human-machine conceptualized?

Concepts of sociality in human-machine interaction particularly draw on Anglo-American approaches to the social and behavioral sciences. In these approaches sociality is regarded as the outcome of the interaction of individuals, which is understood primarily as self-interested. Hence, "'social' refers to the exchange of costs and benefits in the pursuit of outcomes of purely personal value, and 'society' is the aggregate of individuals in pursuit of their respective self-interests." (Caporael 1995: 1)

These (reductionist) concepts are partly translated into the design of social robots and software agents. The models often become even more trivialized and simplified through software implementation processes. For example, in software agent research human behavior is commonly standardized by no more than five personality traits and six basic emotions.

Concepts of human-machine relationship, particularly in the new field of 'social' AI illustrate further ontological and anthropological assumptions. The relationships of owner-pet, parent-baby or caregiver-infant are sorts of pedagogical relationships that afford a lot of time, patience, engagement and work in order to function properly. Are these the kind of relationships desirable for human-machine interaction? Do we really want to educate our machines?

To summarize and to return to our starting question about the strategies, which are necessary to design 'de-gendered technologies', we argue that a deconstruction of gender representation as well as a critique of fundamental epistemological and ontological assumptions are essential. The criterion for promising research in this field cannot be the question whether guidelines for an alternative technology design are provided. Instead such an approach aims at a fundamental revision of societal structures, politics of representation *and* technoscientific discourses and practices.

References

Adam, Alison (1998): Artificial Knowing, Gender and the Thinking Machine. London/New York: Routledge.

Becker, Barbara (1992): Künstliche Intelligenz. Konzepte, Systeme, Verheißungen. Frankfurt am Main: Campus.

Breazeal, Cynthia (2002): Designing Sociable Robots. Cambridge, Mass.: MIT Press.

Cassell, Justine; Sullivan, Joseph; Prevost, Scott; Churchill, Elizabeth (2000): Embodied Conversational Agents. Cambridge, Mass.: MIT Press.

Caporael, Linnda R. (1995): Sociality: Coordinating Bodies, Minds and Groups. Psycoloquy 6 (01), Groupselection 1. Available: http://psycprints.ecs.soton.ac.uk/archive/00000448. Accessed January 18, 2006.

Crutzen, Cecile (2003): ICT-Representations as transformative critical rooms. In: Kreutzner, Gabriele; Schelhowe, Heidi (eds): Agents of Change. Virtuality, Gender and the Challenge to the Traditional University. Opladen: Leske + Budrich: 87-106.

Collins, Harry (1990): Artificial Experts. Social Knowledge and Intelligent Machines. Cambridge, Mass.: MIT Press.

Dreyfus, Hubert (1963): What Computers Can't Do. A Critique of Artificial Reason. New York: Harper & Row.

Duffy, Brian (2003): Anthropomorphism and the Social Robot. In: Robotics and Autonomous Systems 42 (3-4): 177-190. (See also online. Available: http://www.cs.ucd.ie/csprism/publications/desire/IROS-AnthroSocialRobot.pdf. Accessed January 18, 2006).

Fausto-Sterling, Anne (1985): Myths of Gender, Biological Theories about Women and Men. New York: Basic Books.

Fong, Terrence; Nourbakhsh, Illah; Dautenhahn, Kerstin (2003): A Survey of Socially Interactive Robots. In: Robotics and Autonomous Systems 42 (3-4): 235-243.

Gratch, Jonathan; Rickel, Jeff; André, Elisabeth; Cassell, Justine; Petajan, Eric; Badler, Norman I. (2002): Creating Interactive Virtual Humans: Some Assembly Required. In: IEEE Intelligent Systems 17 (4): 54-63.

Heintz, Bettina (1995): Papiermaschinen. Die sozialen Voraussetzungen maschineller Intelligenz. In: Rammert, Werner (ed.): Soziologie und künstliche Intelligenz. Produkte und Probleme einer Hochtechnologie. Frankfurt am Main: Campus: 37–64.

Hubbard, Ruth (1979): Have Only Men Evolved? In: Hubbard, Ruth; Henifin, Mary Sue; Fried, Barbara (eds): Women Look at Biology Looking At Women: A Collection of Feminist Critiques. Cambridge: Schenkman Publ. Comp. 7-35.

Latour, Bruno (1987): Science in Action. How to Follow Scientists and Engineers through Society. Cambridge: Havard University Press.

Moldt, Daniel; von Scheve, Christian (2002): Attribution and Adaption: the Case of Social Norms and Emotions in Human-Agent Interaction. In: Marsh, Stephen; Nowell, Lucy; Meech, John F.; Dautenhahn, Kerstin (eds): Proceedings of The Philosophy and Design of Socially Adept Technologies, Workshop held in conjunction with CHI'02, 20.4.2002, Minneapolis/Minnesota, USA: 39-41.

Pfeifer, Rolf; Scheier, Christian (1999): Understanding Intelligence. Cambridge, Mass.: MIT Press.

Sengers, Phoebe (1999): Practices for Machine Culture. A Case Study in Integrating Cultural Studies and Artificial Intelligence. In: Surfaces, Volume VIII.

Suchman, Lucy (1987): Plans and Situated Action. The Problem of Human-Machine Communication. Cambridge: Cambridge University Press.

Suchman, Lucy (in prep.): Replicants and Irreductions: Affective Encounters at the Interface. In: Suchman, Lucy: Plans and Situated Actions, 2nd Ed. Cambridge: Cambridge University Press.

Stern, Andrew (2002): Creating Emotional Relationships with Virtual Characters. In: Trappl, Robert; Petta, Paolo; Payr, Sabine (eds): Emotions in Humans and Artifacts, MIT Press, Cambridge, Mass.: 333-362.

Wegner, Peter (1997): Why Interaction Is More Powerful than Algorithms, Communications of the ACM 40 (5): 80-91.

Ambient Intelligence, between Heaven and Hell. A Transformative Critical Room?

Cecile K. M. Crutzen

1 The Short Term Future of Ambient Intelligence

With the theme Ambient Intelligence (AmI) industry, designers and scientists explore a vision of future daily life – a vision of humans being accompanied and surrounded by computerised devices, intelligent interfaces, wireless networking technology and software agents. Computing resources and computing services will be present everywhere and interconnected anytime. The focus of AmI is to bring to life the everyday objects and tools of our daily environment. The purposes of this technology are circumambient ways of monitoring the actions of humans and the changes in their environment. Sensors of many types and physical actors will be used to react and pre-act in a way that is articulated as desirable and pleasant. AmI as a 'crossover approach' is strongly related to several other Computer Science topics (Punie 2003: 6; Schmidt 2004; Oulasvirta 2004). This technology is not new. A lot of ambient technology is already available, like monitoring analogue physical processes, describing them with digital data and analysing these data using knowledge-based interpretation models. New is that the public and the private environment of humans is permeated by an overwhelming number of autonomous active devices. This will cause the inevitability of the employment of artificial intelligent agents to automate routine decisions and to provide against stupefying read and write collisions[15] of the artificial devices. There is no guarantee that these artificial agents can cooperate appropriately and safely. This penetration process has already started with remote recognition systems for facial expression and body tracking (Turk 2004). With biometrics technology our hands, eyes, voices, faces and movements will be used to control the way we live (Jain 2004; Oviatt 2004).

---

15   Intelligent agents pick up and send data to and from other agents in their environment (read and write). These data can get mixed up; agents receive not intended data or send data to not intended other agents. In the future anti-collision facilities are needed e.g. in the agents themselves or in separate agents meant to protect the individual or the community from unintended infiltrations.

In the very near future humans will be overwhelmed by huge quantities of personalised real-time responses based for instance on networking RFID tags.[16] AmI implies a seamless environment of computing, advanced networking technology and specific (mainly remote and non tangible) computer interfaces for humans.[17] In the future AmI will influence the modelling[18] of how people should live in a community. At the moment, the main effort of the AmI industry is towards designing simple isolated appliances that might be acceptable to consumers of this new technology. This prepares the ground for a complete infiltration of our environment with even more intelligent and interconnected devices. People should become familiar with AmI; slowly and unspectacularly; getting used to handing over the initiative to artificial devices. A lot of sensing infrastructure has already been installed for handling security and road traffic. What remains to be done is to shift the domain of the intended monitoring just enough to feed the ongoing process of people getting used to these controls and forgetting the embarrassment of being permanently monitored, in other words – having no off-switch.

Questioning gender in AmI could be an appropriate way to investigate the assumptions within the AmI discourse. Is AmI a technology that destabilises the fixed meaning of gender or will AmI stabilise the existing networks? Perhaps we can find answers if we analyse the visions of industry and designers, their justifications lying in security and care needs. Questioning gender needs a deconstruction of the relation between "use" and "design" in AmI products. Will AmI strengthen the opposition of use and design that is strongly related to gender?

2   The Visions of Industry and Designers

The characteristics of AmI in many promotional publications are that smart objects will make our whole lives relaxed and enjoyable (Philips Research 2003). There are many attractive scenarios for the individual that represent a heaven on earth full of enjoyment. The AmI industry offers a service of personalisation. AmI is tailored to your needs and it can recognise you everywhere. As you move through an environment, AmI interfaces register your presence, self-initiatively perform tasks designed to make your life easier, and learn from your behaviour

---

16   RFID (radio frequency identification): A generic term for technologies that use radio waves to remotely identify people or objects carrying reactive tags. See e.g. http://www.rfidjournal.com/article/articleview/207 Accessed April 2, 2005, or McGinity (2004).
17   Named 'implicit HCI' in Schmidt (2004: 164).
18   E.g. the modelling of interaction patterns of humans that are imbedded in the functionalities of AmI-products.

in order to anticipate your future needs. The promises of intelligent adaptability and anticipation are directed to the individual. AmI 'will be capable of meeting needs' and anticipating and responding intelligently to spoken or gestured wishes and desires without conscious mediation, and even these could result in systems that are capable of engaging in 'intelligent dialogue' (Punie 2003: 5). AmI designers see themselves as the creators of a better future; working along a straight line of civilising progress. They speak like heavenly fathers, creating a technological paradise, sensitive and responsive to people's vision of heaven on earth. They follow the ideal of creating devices, which cause no disturbances and fit perfectly with their assumed expectations. AmI designers are convinced that digital environments, by acting on people's behalf, can improve of people's quality of life.[19] 'Good' design is defined as making a product, which will not create disharmony or doubt in the life of its users. Their concept of 'usercentredness' is based on a notion of non-problematic interaction: '... which means technology that can think on its own and react to (or possibly even predict) individual needs so people don't have to work to use it'.[20] In such statements many subjective decisions on 'what is a better and easier life' are made. Having an 'easier life', meaning no time consuming distractions and no unnecessary disturbances, is considered to be progress.[21] This connection between technology and progress undervalues the subjectivity and situatedness of progress. It is very questionable as to whether or not human life will be better if artificial actors purposefully manipulate our behaviour and eventually gain control over it[22].

3   The Justification for AmI: Security and Care

One interpretation of the meaning of 'a better life' is 'taking away the worries' of a possibly unstable future. People are made vulnerable and naked without an artificial skin of input and output devices. Single-purpose AmI applications will

---

19   The Ambience project: http://www.extra.research.philips.com/euprojects/ambience/ Accessed April, 2, 2005.
20   Philips Sustainability Report (2002), www.philips.com/Assets/Downloadablefile/sustainability -2153.pdf Accessed April, 2, 2005.
21   European Foundation for the Improvement of Living and Working Conditions, sector future (2003): The future of IT – now it's getting personal, http://www.emcc.eurofound.eu.int/publi-cations/2003/sf_ict_1.pdf Accessed April, 2, 2005.
22   E.g. if you are a heart patient, you will be forced to use a device that will register your smoking and eating behaviour. The next step could be that the insurance companies will refuse to pay for your treatment if your behaviour is not appropriate enough for a heart patient in the opinion of the insurance company.

be connected for continuous monitoring of the individual with the strong suggestion that this provides security and maintains health (Friedewald 2003):

> "We trust less and we fear more. We will therefore be searching for reassurance and guarantees. (...) We will welcome tools that allow us to monitor the health of ourselves or our loved ones, that allow quick links with emergency services, or 'tag' our children so that we know where they are. In short how can our technologies look after us and our environments rather than us looking after our technology." (Philips Research 2003: 35)

So domestication of AmI will be forced by jumping on the bandwagon of some fundamental fears of the individual and society. These fears are e.g. the present loss of security and safety because of terrorism, the necessary but unaffordable amount of care needed for the elderly (Braun 2004) and the sick, handling the complexity of combining professional and home work, difficulties in coping with the overwhelming amount and obtrusiveness of interactions and information in our society and being dependent on the gridlocked transport system. So-called 'Killer' applications are largely based on providing a bit more security and safety for the individual (Wahlster 2004). Industries focus, too, on substitutes and prostheses for the human touch in the care of children, the elderly and the disabled:

> "When daily contact is not feasible, the decision to move a senior is often driven by fear and uncertainty for his or her daily well-being. Our goal is to create a surrogate support system that resurrects this informal daily communication." (Mynatt 2001: 340).

Is it enough to outline health care scenarios 'to encompass societal, economic as well as technology developments and form a logical framework in which use cases can be fitted'? Is the goal 'managed care' in a health care system 'that uses organizational and management controls to offer patients appropriate care in cost-effective treatment settings' to the benefit of the patients (Riva 2003: 298)?[23] Can we counter-balance the risk of dehumanisation and depersonalisation by progressively disembodying patients, by reducing them to the sum of their biological and physiological functions and by identifying them with the collection of their vital parameters (Gaggioli 2003: 84)? In particular, it is not enough to offer ordinary people, the consumers of the health industry, control only with an off-switch within their reach, with the argument that these techno-

---

23   See for a similar (potential) effect of technology developments on human relations: Bath and Weber, this volume.

logies could very easily acquire the appearance of 'them controlling us'. Ambient Technology will no doubt control us, but in a situation where people are dependent on health care, for most of them a visible off-switch is not relevant. What is relevant is the availability of human-quality care as good as and as accessible as the intelligent prosthetic care.

All in all, the development of AmI is and will be justified for several medical and ecological reasons and reasons of security. But these valid reasons should not lead us to shut our eyes to the ready-made abuse that could result from AmI.

4   Questioning gender

The meaning of gender is, and always will be, embedded in social, cultural and material constructions and is always dynamically linked to the meaning of many concepts such as technology or the constructed relationship between use and design of technology.[24] AmI will influence the meaning of gender because it will be embedded in those daily environments in which specific gender meanings from the past are reinforced. These performances of gender are mostly symbols or representations of power relations in a domain[25].

Questioning gender is about taking an active, critical role in the technological design of our daily behaviour. It is necessary to influence the process of AmI domestication, because of its impact especially on our routine activities and creative strategies. It is urgent because industry claims that they apply female values and translate these into 'ease of use', 'experience of use', 'less complexity and more simplicity' (Manning 2002). This ease of use is based on the assumption that a perfect adaptability of the artificial devices for humans in their environments is possible and desirable. Questioning gender in AmI is asking: Could AmI be a technology that destabilises the fixed meaning of gender or will AmI stabilise the existing networks?

In scenarios focussed on the individual, human life is idealised and opti-

---

24   The performance of gender in AmI can become visible through questioning and doubting: What has been overvalued, what has been undervalued and what has been ignored? Doubt can occur by criticizing the constructed meaning of activities, which we humans call design-, and use-activities, which are linked to gender in the discourse of the AmI.

25   The hierarchical opposition 'use-design' is linked to other oppositions such as 'technical-human', 'hard-soft', 'secure-doubtful'. These gendered symbolic links are established and re-enforced through the military, mathematical and technological traditions of the Computer Science discipline and through concepts of female Computer Science based on essentialist and deterministic views on femininity and technology.

mised; a 'better life' is visualised. Social issues are only mentioned from an egocentric point of view (Punie 2003: 6; IST Advisory Group 2001). These scenarios are extrapolations from the present, based on the designers' view of what should be better in their own lives. For industry and research these scenarios function as springboards for ideas about what kind of developments, technologies, society, economy, and markets are necessary to arrive at these scenarios. Describing scenarios is not an innocent activity. [26] Incorporating the gender matrix of dualism is unavoidable because it is a repetition of present-day beliefs. Scenarios are indicative and normative, they form the foundations of political decisions, which research topics will be financed and which not, which applications will be developed and which not. So scenarios for a 'better life' for the prototypical individual might become the standard way of living for everyone. In official EU scenarios like 'Maria' and 'Dimitrios' (IST Advisory Group 2001)[27], who are both portrayed as very busy western people with almost no private life, the scenario-problem becomes evident. Questioning gender in AmI is asking whose lives are being represented and whose not?

The convergence of the designed domestication processes based on the assumption of a 'better life' could become an apocalyptic trip of an automatic 'repression to normality', without the option of creative adventures or explorations. Why is it that in these scenarios it is only the advantages of AmI that are raised?

What underlies the assumption that Ambient Intelligence will, by disappearing into our environment, bring humans both an easy and entertaining life? How can we see through the dazzling performances of smart and aesthetically designed objects, homes[28] and environments? How can we make scientists and designers take responsibility for not placing enough importance on privacy, cultural diversity and other ethical issues? Simply mentioning ethical issues at the end of a conference paper is an unacceptable substitute for failing to take on this responsibility.[29] Questioning gender means questioning responsibilities.

---

26   For a critique of scenarios see also Giráldez (2004: 274)
27   An animated scenario for 'Anya' (corporate creative knowledge worker who works equally from home, the office and whilst travelling; she has one teenage son, Paul, from her previous marriage to Joe and a four year old daughter, Minnie, with her current partner, Marcus) is to be found at http://www.eurescom.de/public/projects/P1300-series/P1302/ Accessed April, 2, 2005.
28   For an overview on smart homes see under topic 'Smart Rooms, Smart Houses & Household Appliances' of the American Association for Artificial Intelligence (AAAI) http://www.aaai.org/ AITopics/html/rooms.html Accessed April, 2, 2005.
29   This is mostly the case in publications in which the technological realisations are highlighted. For instance, in (Riva 2004) ethical and social aspects have a prominent place. See also for social implications: Raisinghani 2004; Bohn 2002a, 2002b; IST Advisory Group 2002.

'Questioning gender' implies a deconstruction of the oppositions that exist in the discourses of Ambient Intelligence designers, the ICT industry and computer scientists (Crutzen 2005). A deconstruction of the use-design opposition and the progress and care pretensions related to this technology, reveals the power relations within the promotion and realisation of AmI. This could be the beginning of an articulation of the meaning of diversity in the discourses of AmI: diversity in use, in design and in the interaction between use and design. It is a gender question to ask what price humans have to pay in the end by giving personal, including physical, data to facilitate the action of a surrounding technology. Is it still possible to resist and to distrust the overwhelming promises of a better life?

5   Use and Design

A closer look at the relationship humans have constructed with their environment, at how humans experience the things and tools in their environment, is necessary to analyse the influence of AmI. Actions and interactions always cause changes, but not all activities of actors are 'present' in interaction worlds. If changes are comparable and compatible with previous changes, they will be perceived as obvious and taken for granted. The change from a closed door to an open door normally is mentally invisible. Opening and closing the door is in most situations an unreflective act. The door is 'ready-to-hand' and subordinate to the action for which it is used: entering or leaving a room. These ready-to-hand interactions will not raise any doubts. The claim of mental invisibility by AmI is that AmI will be settled in our fixed routines. Marc Weiser [30]was one of the first who focussed on this characterisation of computer technology: 'The most profound technologies are those that disappear. They weave themselves into the fabric of everyday life until they are indistinguishable from it.' (Weiser 1991). Mental invisibility is seen as a precondition for acceptance; the stabilisation of use and the domestication of AmI technology. Mental invisibility can only be the outcome of an integration process on the part of human actors. Things, tools and technologies can become obvious. Humans use them without thinking in their routine acting. But this is only one way of dealing with technology. Not all our acting is routine acting. Using an ICT-product is negotiating, not only about its content, but also about what actions of the ICT-product are suitable for the actor's situation. In my opinion translations and

---

30   Mark Weiser (1952 - 1999) was a chief scientist of Xerox PARC and widely considered to be the father of Ubiquitous computing and Calm technology.

replacements of ICT-representations should not fit smoothly without conflict into the world for which they are made ready. A closed readiness is an ideal, which is not feasible, because in the interaction situation the acting itself of human actors is partly ad-hoc and therefore unpredictable. The ready-made behaviour and the content of ICT-representations should then be differentiated and changeable to enable users to make ICT-representations ready and reliable for their own spontaneous and creative use.

Doubt is a necessary precondition for changing the pattern of interaction itself. According to Heidegger, the 'present-at-handness' (Vorhandenes) and the 'ready-to-handness' (Zuhandenes) of a tool are situated and they do not exclude each other. On the contrary, they offer the option of intertwining use and design activities in interaction with the tool itself. This intertwining makes a tool reliable, because it is always individual and situated.[31] According to Dourish, this can happen only through involved, embodied interaction. Intertwining of use and design needs the present-at-hand of the ICT-representations (Dourish 2001: 125). Their readiness-to-hand should be doubtable. In a lot of AmI applications, you are not the initiator of the action anymore. Your body data are used for actions of physical invisible artificial actors, e.g. are you always aware of security systems, observing you? The number of examples of applications that are closely tied to your habits and that consequently stabilise and freeze those habits, is growing. Hence, these applications no longer give you the opportunity to change your behaviour as they are surrounding you and becomementally invisible.

Humans needs transformative critical rooms[32] as spaces where the inter-actions take place between human actors and ICT-representations and their interpretation can be negotiated and where doubt can occur as a constructive strategy. Creating these rooms requires actors who already have a habit of causing doubt and who accept that truths are always situated. In this interaction the meaning of "use" is reconstructed. Using ICT representations imply the (re)design of a flexible environment where the connection between human and non-human actors can always be disconnected. The activities of use and design occur simultaneously as an ongoing process where change takes place and where

---

31   Tools can be a part of our habits. They exit in our unreflective BACKGROUND, Heidegger calls this ready to hand. At the same time tools can have the possibility of discovering, reconstruct their meaning within a structure of reference. They become present again. (Capurro 1992: 367).
      For a definition of 'present at hand' and 'ready to hand' see (Heidegger 1926, §15, §16.): http://www.lancs.ac.uk/depts/philosophy/awaymave/405/glossary.htm Accessed April, 2, 2005 and (Svanæs 1999: 45-46; Dourish 1999: 12; Dourish, 2001: 106-110; Crutzen 2003)

32   Critical means that doubt about the behaviour of yourself and of the surrounding human and non-human actors is possible. Transformative means that out of doubt, change of the interaction patterns is possible. (Crutzen 2003, Crutzen 2006 a,b)

actability[33] becomes an important condition. (Crutzen 2003: Crutzen, Kotkamp, 2006a,b)

6   The transformative critical room of AmI

AmI is a pattern of models of interaction chains embedded in things. Objects in our daily world – mostly inanimate – will be enriched by an intelligence that will make them almost 'subjects', capable of responding to stimuli from the world around them and even of anticipating the stimuli. In the AmI world the 'relationship' between us and the technology around us is no longer one of a user towards a machine or tool, but of a person towards an 'object-became-subject', something that is capable of reacting and of being educated.[34] Everyday objects such as doors, tables, books, lights or even the flow of air and water are transformed into computational interfaces (Ishii 1998). It is a future of artificial actors 'whispering' in the background of human life and awareness, interacting with each other and their environment. People become the objects of the ongoing 'conversations'. In the vision of industrial designers AmI is embedded; many invisible distributed devices are hidden in the environment. A continuous process of miniaturisation of mechatronic systems and components will make this possible. Physical invisibility or perceptual invisibility mean that one cannot sense (smell, see, hear or touch) the AmI devices anymore; one cannot sense their presence nor sense their full (inter-)action, but only that part of interaction output that was intended to change the environment of the individual user. Many (inter-)actions between artificial devices will take place in the background of the life of the individual. According to Schmidt, our relationship to computer systems will change from 'explicit interaction that requires always a kind of dialogue between the user and a particular system or computer, …to implicit interaction'. (Schmidt 2004: 162, 166). The physical disappearance of AmI from our environment means that the whole environment surrounding the individual has the potential to function as an interface.

---

33   Actability: human actors can experience other actors as 'actable' if these actors present themselves in a way, which is interpretable out of their own experiences. That does not mean that this is the intended interpretation of the designers because each actor has her or his horizon of experiences and expectations. Tools and things are actable, if humans can give meaning to them by drawing them into their interactions. A necessary condition of actability of artificial tools is that humans can perceive the performance of the artificial devices.

34   Statement by Stefano Marzano in 'newvaluenews number thirteen – Philips Design – July 2002': 16 http://www.design.philips.com/assets/Downloadablefile/New_value_News13-12820.pdf Accessed April, 2, 2005

The overvaluation of 'design' by designers, industry and research in AmI has reduced 'design within use' to themes such as 'the adaptability of the technology' and 'the acceptance of these technologies by users'. The price of the promised adaptability of these intelligent devices is continuous measurement and interpretation of our body[35] data and movements (Noldus 2003)

This opening up of the private lives of AmI users is accompanied by closing off more and more opportunities for users to adjust AmI devices to protect themselves from unwanted actions. The price will be that the users will be limited in the options available to them to articulate their wishes and experience doubt. People are in danger of losing within the activity of use the activity of 'design'. In AmI the symbolic meaning of use and design is reconstructed as an opposition in which 'design' is active and a virtuoso activity and 'use' is passive and not creative. This dominance of design discloses and largely prevents the act of discovery of the users by the designer[36] and acts of discovery on the part of the users. Design is focused on generalised and classified users. Users are turned into resources, which can be used by designers in the process of making ICT-products. They do not have sufficient room for starting their own design processes. Those who do not fit into regimented classes are seen as dissidents. In AmI, designers are creating an artificial play in which they have given the active and leading role to the artificial subjects. Users are ready-made sources of data for the technology in their environment. Placing the user at the centre of AmI design contradicts the view that AmI technology should be mentally and physically invisible and unobtrusive. By interpreting 'usercentredness' in this way, the active explicit participation aspect is lost. In the architectural concept of AmI of Piva et al., the user is reduced to an observable object placed in a feedback loop that converges to an optimal intelligent environment with an action/communication oriented smart space function in order to influence the user (Piva et al. 2005).

7   Conclusion of the Deconstruction: Critical Transformative Rooms

In the future AmI things and tools will be unavoidable. Western high-tech-society is developing into a world inhabited by cyborgs. However, can humans

---

35   Rejane Cantoni calls the related research platform 'Bodyarchitecture': '... for investigating different forms of natural, multimodal human-computer interaction. It involves the research and development of computer vision, speech and gesture recognition systems that connect media and physical spaces to what its inhabitants are, and do and say.' (Cantoni 2005)

36   In AmI environments humans become resources. They are reduced to objects; only providers of data which will function as input for the acting of the AmI environment.

in AmI environments still act as cyborgs in the sense of Haraway, living in a symbiotic relationship with the machines, staying responsible for them by '... embracing the skilful task of reconstructing the boundaries of daily life', by '... building and destroying machines, identities, categories, relationships, space, stories ...' (Haraway 1991: 180-181)? Can the cyborg image construct a way out of the maze of dualisms or should instead the cyborg be interpreted as an actor in the middle of these dualisms, creating critical transformative rooms: places in which, by questioning the performance of gender, the underlying ontological and epistemological assumptions of the actors (industry, designers, users) in the domain of AmI could be analysed? Is there still time to escape from the powerful push of the industry to introduce this all-enveloping server-technology? Is it still possible to claim technology should be used under human conditions, where things that are technically possible are no longer necessarily seen as progress? Perhaps Haraway was right in her claim to be a cyborg rather than a goddess, because the technological heaven is an illusion.

In the process of a critical domestication of AmI technology, acting within the AmI-induced dualisms users should feel not only the comfort of being permanently cared for, but also the pain of giving away intimacy. We should feel that danger, but in feeling it should not be clueless. The critical transformative room that stands between the consumer and AmI should include a diversity of options to influence the behaviour, use and design of the technology. The off-switch is only one end of a rich spectrum of possible intervention tools. Petersen thinks that the technology should reveal at least what the system has to offer in order to motivate users to relate the possibilities of the technology to their actual needs, dreams and wishes. 'For this purpose, domestic technologies should be remarkable rather than unremarkable' (Petersen 2004: 1446).

Designers and researchers feel this pain, too, but they compensate for this by the hard to beat satisfaction of building this technology.[37] The core of their attraction to this lies in 'I can make it', 'It is possible' and 'It works'. It is the technically possible and makeable that always gets the upper hand. Who wants to belong to the non-designers? (Sloterdijk 2001: 375). A gender deconstruction of AmI should lead to a reconstruction of the AmI technology in which users are the actors and designers of their own environments in a critical transformative way.

---

37   The pain of losing privacy or losing your own identity is the same for users and designers. However designers can suppress these feelings; overwhelmed by the kick of making a technology that works.

References

Bohn, Jürgen; Coroama, Vlad; Langheinrich, Marc; Mattern, Friedemann; Rohs, Michael (2002b): Living in a World of Smart Everyday Objects - Social, Economic, and Ethical Implications. Available: http://www.vs.inf.ethz.ch/publ/papers/hera.pdf. Accessed April 2, 2005.

Braun, Anette; Constantelou, Anastasia; Karounou, Vasiliki; Ligtvoet, Andreas; Burgelman, Jean-Claude; Cabrera, Marcelino (2004): eHealth in the context of a European Ageing Society. Available: http://esto.jrc.es/detailshort.cfm?ID_report= 1207. Accessed December 30, 2004.

Cantoni, Rejane (2005): Bodyarchitecture: the Evolution of Interface towards Ambient Intelligence. In: Riva et al. (2005): 213-219. Available: http://www.vepsy.com/ communication/book5/11_AMI_Cantoni.pdf. Accessed April 2, 2005.

Capurro, Rafael (1992): Informatics and Hermeneutic. In: Floyd, Christiane; Keil-Slawik, Reinhard; Budde, Reinhard; Züllighoven, Heinz (eds): Software Development and Reality Construction. Berlin: Springer Verlag: 363-375.

Crutzen, Cecile. K.M. (2003): ICT-Representations as Transformative Critical Rooms. In: Kreutzner, Gabriele; Schelhowe, Heidi (eds): Agents of Change: Virtuality, Gender, and the Challenge to the Traditional University. Leske+Budrich: Opladen: 87-106.

Crutzen, Cecile. K.M. (2005): Intelligent Ambience between Heaven and Hell. In: Archibald, Jaqueline; Emms, Judy; Grundy, Frances; Payne, Janet; Turner, Eva (eds): The Gender Politics of ICT. Middlesex University Press: 29-50.

Crutzen, Cecile. K.M; Kotkamp, Erna (2006a): Questioning gender through transformative critical rooms. In: Trauth, Eileen (ed.): Encyclopedia of Gender and Information Technology. Hershey, PA: Idea Group Reference.

Crutzen, Cecile. K.M.; Kotkamp, Erna (2006b): Questioning gender through Deconstruction and Doubt. In: Trauth, Eileen (ed.): Encyclopedia of Gender and Information Technology. Hershey, PA: Idea Group Reference.

Dourish, Paul (1999): Embodied Interaction: Exploring the Foundations of a New Approach. Available: http://www.dourish.com/embodied/embodied99.pdf. Accessed April 2, 2005.

Dourish, Paul (2001): Where the Action is. Cambridge: The MIT Press.

Friedewald, Michael; Costa, Olivier Da (2003): Science and Technology Roadmapping: Ambient Intelligence in Everyday Life (AmI@Life). Available: http://esto.jrc.es/ docs/AmIReportFinal.pdf. Accessed March 29, 2006.

Gaggioli, Andrea; Vettorello, Marco; Giuseppe, Riva (2003): From Cyborgs to Cyberbodies: The Evolution of the Concept of Techno-Body in Modern Medicine. In: PsychNology Journal 1 (2): 75-86. Available: http://www.psychology.org/File/ PSYCHOLOGY_JOURNAL_1_2_GAGGIOLI.pdf. Accessed April 2, 2005.

Giráldez, Marcelino Cabrera; Casal, Carlos Rodríguez (2005): The Role of Ambient Intelligence in the Social Integration of the Elderly. In: Riva et al.: 267- 282.

Haraway, Donna J. (1991): A Cyborg Manifesto: Science, Technology and Social-Feminism in the late Twentieth Century. In: Haraway, Donna J.: Simians, Cyborgs, and Women. The Reinvention of Nature. London: Free Association Books.

Heidegger, Martin (1926): Sein und Zeit. Used edition: Heidegger, Martin: Sein und Zeit. Tübingen, Niemeyer: 17. Auflage, 1993.

Ishii, Hiroshi; Wisneski, Craig; Brave, Scott; Dahley, Andrew; Gorbet, Matt; Ullmer, Brygg; Yarin, Paul (1998): ambientROOM: integrating ambient media with architectural space. CHI 98 conference summary on Human factors in computing systems. April 18-23, 1998, Los Angeles, California, United States: 173-174.

IST Advisory Group (2001): Scenarios for Ambient Intelligence in 2010, edited by: Ducatel, Ken; Bogdanowicz, Marc; Scapolo, Fabiana; Burgelman, Jean-Claude. IPTS-ISTAG, EC: Luxembourg. Available: ftp://ftp.cordis.lu/pub/ist/docs/istagscenarios2010.pdf. Accessed April 2, 2005.

IST Advisory Group (2002): IST Advisory Group - Trust, Dependability, Security and Privacy for IST in FP6. Available: ftp://ftp.cordis.lu/pub/ist/docs/istag-securitywg61final0702.pdf. Accessed April 2, 2005.

Jain, Anil K.; Ross, Arun (2004): Multibiometric Systems, In: Communications of the ACM 47 (1): 34-44.

Manning, Andre (2002): Research into women's impact on technology. In: Philips News 2002. Available: http://www.newscenter.philips.com/about/news/section-13488/article-2235.html. Accessed April 2, 2005.

McGinity, Meg (2004): RFID: is this game of tag fair play? In: Communications of the ACM 47 (1): 15-18.

Mynatt, Elizabeth D.; Rowan, Jim; Craighill, Sarah; Jacobs, Annie (2001): Digital family portraits: Supporting Peace of Mind for Extended Family Members. In: Proceedings of the ACM Conference on Human Factors in Computing Systems (CHI 2001), Seattle, Washington: ACM Press: 333-340. Available: http://www.cc.gatech.edu/fce/ecl/projects/dfp/pubs/dfp-chi2001.pdf. Accessed April 2, 2005.

Noldus, Lucas (2003): HomeLab as a Scientific Measurement and Analysis Instrument. In: Philips Research: 27-29.

Oulasvirta, Antti; Salovaara, Antti (2004): A Cognitive Meta-Analysis of Design Approaches to Interruptions in Intelligent Environments. In: CHI 2004, April 24-29, 2004, Vienna, Austria, Late Breaking Results Paper: 1155-1158.

Oviatt, Sharon; Darrell, Trevor; Flickner Myron (eds) (2004): Multimodal interfaces that flex, adapt, and persist. In: Communications of the ACM 47 (1) 30-33.

Petersen, Marianne Graves (2004): Remarkable Computing - the Challenge of Designing for the Home. In: CHI 2004, April 24-29, Vienna, Austria: 1445-1448.

Philips Research (2003): 365 days - Ambient Intelligence research in HomeLab. Available: http://www.research.philips.com/technologies/misc/homelab/downloads/homelab_365.pdf. Accessed April 2, 2005.

Piva, Stefano; Singh, Reetu; Gandetto, Matteo; Regazzoni, Carlo S. (2005): A Context-based Ambient Intelligence Architecture. In: Remagnino et al.: 63-87.

Punie, Yves (2003): A social and technological view of Ambient Intelligence in Everyday Life: What bends the trend? Key Deliverable, The European Media and Technology in Everyday Life Network, 2000-2003, Institute for Prospective Technological Studies, Directorate General Joint Research Centre, European Commission. Available: http://www.lse.ac.uk/collections/EMTEL/reports/punie_2003_emtel.pdf. Accessed April 2, 2005.

Raisinghani, Mahesh S. (2004): Ambient Intelligence: Changing Forms of Human-Computer Interaction and Their Social Implications. In: Journal of Digital Information 5 (4), Article No. 271, 2004-08-24. http://jodi.ecs.soton.ac.uk/Articles/v05/i04/Raisinghani/. Accessed April 2, 2005.

Remagnino, Paola; Foresti, Gian Luca; Ellis, Tim (eds) (2005): Ambient Intelligence: A Novel Paradigm. Springer, New York.

Riva, Giuseppe (2003): Ambient Intelligence in Health Care. In: Cyberpsychology & Behavior: 6 (3). Available: http://labstudenti.unicatt.it/doo/autori/Username%20n.% 2007/p295_s.pdf, pp.295-300. Accessed April 2, 2005.

Riva, Giuseppe; Vatalaro, Francesco; Davide, Fabrizio; Alcañiz, Mariano (eds) (2005): Ambient Intelligence. IOS Press. Available: http://www.emergingcommunication.com/volume6.html. Accessed April 2, 2005.

Sloterdijk, Peter (2001): Kränkung durch Maschinen, In: Sloterdijk, Peter: Nicht gerettet. Versuche nach Heidegger. Suhrkamp Verlag, Frankfurt am Main: 338-366.

Schmidt, Albrecht (2005): Interactive Context-Aware Systems Interacting with Ambient Intelligence. In: Riva et al. 2005: 159-178.

Svanæs, Dag (1999): Understanding Interactivity, Steps to a Phenomenology of Human-Computer Interaction. Available: http://www.idi.ntnu.no/~dags/interactivity.pdf. Accessed April 2, 2005.

Turk, Matthew (2004): Computer vision in the interface. In: Communications of the ACM 47 (1): 60-67.

Wahlster, Wolfgang et al. (2004): Grand Challenges in the Evolution of the Information Society. Available: ftp://ftp.cordis.lu/pub/ist/docs/istag_draft_report_grand_challenges_wahlster_06_07_04.pdf. Accessed April 2, 2005.

Weiser, Marc (1991): The Computer for the 21st Century. In: Scientific American: 265 (3): 94-104, reprinted in IEEE: Pervasive Computing, January-March 2002: 19-25. Available: http://www.ubiq.com/hypertext/weiser/SciAmDraft3.html. Accessed April 2, 2005.

Feminist Technoscience Rearranging in the Black Box of Information Technology

Christina Björkman, Pirjo Elovaara, Lena Trojer

"Dozens of feminist writers have refused both relativism and universalism. Subjects, objects, kinds, races, species, genres, and genders are products of their relating. None of this work is about finding sweet and nice – 'feminine' – worlds and knowledges free of the ravages and productivities of power. Rather, feminist inquiry is about understanding how things work, who is in the action, what might be possible, and how worldly actors might somehow be accountable to and love each other less violently." (Haraway 2003: 6)

Introduction

What kind of focus will feminist research develop at a technical university, where information technology (IT)[38] constitutes the overarching research field? In this article we want to illustrate this question with the core issues that we have identified, as well as to animate these with the authors' stories. Finally, we want to propose a short agenda of issues and challenges for future feminist technoscience research.

The first starting point for our article is feminist technoscience, implying attention to issues related to boundaries and boundary crossings between science, technology, politics and society. The feminist technoscience approach has revolved around exploring the epistemological foundations of knowledge understandings and practices – focusing on deconstructions, opening up concepts and definitions. By doing this it has "...visualized science and technology as discourse, but has on the other hand been less good an agent for changing science/technology. Deconstructions have been made, but re-formulations have been less tangible." (Mörtberg 2003: 60) The research group Technoscience Studies, established in 1998 at Blekinge Institute of Technology (BTH), Sweden,

---

38   We have chosen to use the term information technology and its abbreviation IT, since in the Swedish context these are the prevailing concepts, rather than the term Information and Communication Technology (ICT).

engages in research that from feminist technoscience research perspectives aims to develop complex understandings and practices of IT. The crucial challenge is to move beyond the layers of deconstructions, and the core question becomes: how can feminist technoscience research be used for intervention and transformation?

Our second starting point is taken from the notion of IT. First of all, in its Swedish context[39], IT is defined as a technical area. This definition is commonly accepted and used in different fields such as education and occupational training and also in the context of working life. Secondly, when the technical definition of IT is firmly and commonly embedded, or 'blackboxed'[40], the technology itself with its underlying perceptions of technology development and knowledge are seldom brought into focus. One important issue that we see with respect to feminist technoscience research with a focus on IT is the opening and rearranging of this black box, in order to create new approaches, ideas and understandings as well as new possibilities for change. Paraphrasing Sandra Harding's concept of "the science question in feminism", in which she argued for a shift of focus from women in science towards science itself, its foundations, theories and methodologies (Harding 1986), we see feminist technoscience research as constituting a turn towards "the technoscience question in feminism".

The third starting point for this article comes from the authors' lived realities, practices and experience, where smoothness and roughness co-exist and create tensions that both tear and inspire. This for us privileged position provides an opportunity not only to investigate IT from an outside perspective, but as Lucy Suchman, referring to Judy Wajcman, writes: "JW suggests that really to understand these processes of exclusion and resistance, feminist scholars need to get inside the 'black box' of technology production: that there is room for an effective politics around gaining access to technological work and institutions, and that there are, as she puts it, 'opportunities for disruption in the engine rooms of technological production' (Wajcman 1991: 164)" (Suchman 2002: 101). Feminist research should not only be *on* IT as something defined and ready-made, but also an active participation *in* IT research.

We indicate what we identify as core issues by discussing boundaries, challenges and prerequisites for transformations as well as interventions and

---

39   See e.g. Government Bill 1995/96:86 Measures to broaden and develop the use of information
      technology [Regeringens proposition 1995/96:86 *Åtgärder för att öka användning av IT*],
      http://www.regeringen.se [2005-12-12], Government Bill 1999/2000:125 An Information
      Society for All [Regeringens proposition 1999/2000:125 *Ett informationssamhälle för alla*],
      http://www.regeringen.se [2005-12-12].

40   "... blackboxing, a process that makes the joint production of actors and artefacts entirely
      opaque ..." (Latour 1999: 183).

disruptions, both explicitly and more implicitly, in our stories. What happens when feminist technoscience research meets knowledge production and producers in the "engine rooms", including the public and private sectors, development projects, education, academia, and local practices?

After discussing issues concerning boundaries related to university structure and our situation at a technical university, each of us will tell a story about the interventions we have created and/or participated in – interventions that are meant to contribute to re-arrangement in the black box of IT and knowledge production. We conclude the article with a discussion of the issues and challenges we see for feminist technoscience research.

Problematic Boundaries in the "Engine Rooms of Technological Production"

"My experience of the working relations of technology production and use has led among other things to a preoccupation with boundaries, including efforts to recognize them, problematize them, at times maintain them, and at other times to work across them." (Suchman 2002: 93)

Lucy Suchman's words have inspired us to identify categories surrounded by numerous boundaries and to analyse whether the boundaries limit our working and transformation space. Suchman invites us to explore what it would mean to transgress the problematic boundaries.

Boundaries create classifications and categories, spaces to live in and act from. Bowker and Star describe the phenomena and practice of classification: "A classification is a spatial, temporal and spatio-temporal segmentation of the world. A 'classification system' is a set of boxes (metaphorical or literal) into which things [we would like to add: people] can be put to then do some kind of work – bureaucratic or knowledge production... Classifications are consistent and unique, mutually exclusive and complete." (Bowker and Star 1999: 10)

A university is an arrangement based on categories and classifications that fits well into Bowker's and Star's description. In our cartographical work identifying the boundaries and categories inside the technical university, the following four boundary-based categories seem to be the most troublesome and powerful:

- The university structure is based on disciplinary boundaries – difficult and challenging when developing inter- and trans-disciplinary research.
- The university definition and understanding of IT as a hardcore technical category – difficult and challenging when working to broaden the understanding of IT.

- The university category of knowledge is often connected only to the theoretical knowledge produced at academia – difficult to recognise distributed knowledge processes and challenging to respect and co-operate with other knowledge producers outside the university.
- The university as part of the academic world is a closed classification system based on mutually exclusive categories – there is little if any space for change.

Categories and classifications are named, listed and articulated as disciplines, departments, academic titles, professional positions, research areas, etc. These categories provide a repertoire of labels that help to describe oneself and also to find others belonging to the same categories. Smooth orderings and stabilisations. These categories, and boundaries between them, are a living reality, not just constructions, and most tangibly present in attempts at inter-/transdisciplinary work. Lucy Suchman concludes that disciplinary distinctions "all orient not only to different problems but more significantly to different, sometimes incommensurate conceptions of the social/technical world." What hinders us, she says, are "discontinuities across our intellectual and professional traditions and associated practices" (Suchman 2002: 96).

These disciplinary distinctions are responsible for the difficulties and challenges encountered in broadening the understanding of IT, where the issue of knowing within categories is raised: "A crucial assumption underwriting these persistent boundaries is the premise that technical expertise is not only a *necessary*, but is the *sufficient* form of knowledge for the production of new technologies." (Suchman 2002: 93, original italics). Categories are mutually exclusive. If you are placed inside a technological discipline, you cannot at the same time be categorised as a social scientist, and vice versa. Inclusion in one specific category means that you firmly and definitely are outside another category. This leads to an attempt to understand who is outside and who is inside when the borders are drawn, and what it means to be outside and inside, when talking about the power to define and the power to act.

Recognising and living within boundaries makes one wonder how powerful, well protected and stable these boundaries are. Are they transgressable? Contrary to Bowker and Star, Donna Haraway says in an interview: "Categories are not frozen... The world is more lively than that, including us, and there are always more things going on than you thought, maybe less than there should be, but more than you thought!" (Lykke et al. 2000: 55)

Challenging Boundaries

> "...crossing boundaries as a project of mutual learning and partial translation..."
> (Suchman 2002: 93)

What boundaries do we challenge? The group, by its very existence within a technical faculty, challenges the boundaries of what is considered to be technology. As we see it, IT as a field of knowledge and expertise crosses disciplines. However, our experience and our interpretation is that there are forces within the technical domains of IT (such as for example computer science) striving towards disciplinary 'purity' and a narrow, technical definition, where inclusions and exclusions are created and maintained. Our group, by asking questions and studying issues such as "What is IT?", "Who draws the boundaries for what IT is considered to be?", "Why are the boundaries drawn where they are?", "Who is excluded and who is included, and why?", and not least "How could it be different?" challenges such understandings of IT, in an attempt to open and rearrange the black box(es) of IT.

Another boundary transgression comes from what is called experience-based research. Here, research perspectives as well as research questions differ from 'traditional' academic discipline-based research, and challenge the boundaries of what is considered academic research and knowledge production. Our research interests and questions spring from professional experience, either from within or outside academia, i.e. we do not start our research from an a priori academic disciplinary interest. We acknowledge the understanding that contemporary knowledge and technology is increasingly produced in distributed systems, where the boundaries between universities, industry and government are flexible (Gibbons et al. 1994; Nowotny et al. 2001). The definition of knowledge, imperative in western universities, has considered theoretical knowledge as the only form of knowledge. This narrowness excludes above all knowledge understood as "practical intelligence" which is developed and used in concrete situations (see e.g. Göranzon 1991). One of our epistemological foundations is to include not only our own but others' experience-based practical knowledge in our conceptual and practical understanding.

Interventions

In our work, we share and try to develop a common theoretical foundation in feminist epistemologies, as suggested for example by Donna Haraway's notions of situated knowledge and partial perspectives (Haraway 1991). The concept of situated knowledge does not simply refer to a specific place or state, rather it implies a conscious epistemological positioning: "I am arguing for politics and epistemologies of location, positioning, and situating, where partiality and not universality is the condition of being heard to make rational knowledge claims. [...] We do not seek partiality for its own sake, but for the sake of the connections and unexpected openings situated knowledges make possible. The only way to find a larger vision is to be somewhere in particular." (Haraway 1991: 195)

The starting point for our work has been taken from Donna Haraway's epistemological notions, and we use these in different arenas and contexts. We express this as building an epistemological infrastructure for our research, which combines theoretical thinking and intervention practices. Theoretical thinking is a necessary prerequisite for intervention practices, but these practices in turn nurture theoretical thinking. We see this work as our epistemological exercises.

In this section, each of the authors describes and discusses her own project or projects, the experience gained and questions raised by these. The stories may seem disparate, but aim to illustrate the various arenas, and thus possibilities and projects within feminist technoscience. The common denominator is found in the epistemological foundations discussed above, and our projects concern how to bring these epistemological foundations to and use them in transformation work within different practices. The stories are about interventions, our epistemo-logical exercises, which we have created and/or participated in; interventions that were meant to contribute to opening and rearranging the black box(es) of IT and knowledge production.

[Pirjo's Story]

I moved to a university when searching for a space for reflection, believing that it was in academia that knowledge was produced. At the same moment as I crossed the boundary between different practices I also reproduced and accepted the boundary dividing the world into two categories: research producing knowledge and practical work producing services and products. I had moved inside and by so doing I had created an outside that I could observe and write about. At the best moments I could interpret and understand the world outside.

During my research project about local IT-implementations, interviews with librarians forced me to re-think the dividing lines between research and practical work, knowledge production, users and designers of IT. It also forced me to think seriously about my epistemological position, about situatedness and about research (Elovaara 2004). I moved my perspective away from boundaries dividing the world into two separate spaces, to consider the possibility of living and acting beyond the boundaries and looking for a space in between. I also began to consider what kind of research I could conduct in this 'third space' with a desire "to move beyond simple dichotomies" (Suchman 2002: 94).

In 2003 I was able to take my thoughts, dreams, hopes and questions concerning the possibility of this 'third space' research with me to a municipal R&D project defined as an e-democracy project focusing on spatial planning and concentrating on communication and interaction between the municipality and its citizens. The aim of the project was to create a web site, where the new comprehensive municipal spatial plan could be presented and where citizens could comment on the plan and discuss the spatial planning of the future.

The first phase of 'third space' intervention research had to do with transgressing boundaries. In this specific project, transgressing worked in and through multi-perspective intertwined layers. First of all, the actors came from both the public and private sectors. Second, the project was both a research and a development project combining a variety of competencies. And finally, the research part of the project was multidisciplinary[41]. To transgress in order to meet and talk – as easy and uncomplicated activities as these may seem to be – can at the same time uncover the complexity of the transgression. Transgressing is necessary as a start but it is not a guarantee for sustainable change if we do not take into account "the ability partially to translate knowledges among very different – and power-differentiated – communities..." (Haraway 1991: 87).

The second phase of 'third space' intervention research dealt with the general 'noise' caused by the researchers. This noise may consist of a researcher always interrupting people, and taking their time and also taking space. Intervention can also be noise, experienced as disturbance, from even the researcher's point of view. The specific noise during this project was caused by the research group actively participating in the project process. We intervened by arranging workshops and mock-ups[42]. We also caused noise by attending project meetings – not only as passive observers. We did this in order to create space and time for the project participants to think concretely about the project and to work with the design; to blur the boundary between technology development and use. The project was thus a modest contribution to the larger intervention plan, namely to "...begin to replace the designer/user opposition – an opposition that closes off our possibilities for recognizing the subtle and profound differences that actually do divide us – with a rich, densely structured landscape of identities and working relations within which we might begin to move with some

---

41   The notion of multi-disciplinarity indicates the maintenance of discipline boundaries.
42   Workshops to inspire and assist in this specific case the design of the project website.

awareness and clarity regarding our own position." (Suchman 2002: 92)

Finally, members of the research group talked with other members of the project - taking time and disturbing the normal order of working hours. The project leader said that talking with the researchers "costs time. So maybe you cannot say that you directly during the project get anything back to the operative results."[43] We raised issues concerning the notions of democracy and citizenship in discussions. These conversations revealed that project participants did not have similar, harmonious ways of talking about and interpreting democracy and citizenship. A dialogue was opened that sought not final universal definitions of the notions of democracy and citizenship, but local and located interpretations open for problematisations and friction. Negotiations that could be interpreted as provocative – taking a lot of time and producing no direct results – could also be understood as the means by which to localise and situate the essentially contested concepts in a place and time. Or as Lucy Suchman puts it, "The problems that interest us include the practicalities and politics involved in attempting to reconceptualise and restructure the ways in which work and technology design are done." (Suchman et al. 1999: 399) What reconceptualising in the project context meant was that by means of and during the endless number of discussions, the objective was to approach and develop more committed concepts of communication, interaction, democracy and citizenship. The concepts must be situated and accountable as are other members of the project.

Working towards committed concepts takes time and effort. But if the aim of our work is to situate IT and make it sustainable and accountable, one of the goals of feminist technoscience research is to intervene by de- and re-conceptualising our language and experiences. If we aim for committed, situated and "artfully integrated" (Suchman et al. 1999: 99) design, then "this stance of design from nowhere [...], closely tied to the goal of constructing technical systems as commodities that can be stabilised and cut loose from the sites of their production long enough to be exported en masse to the sites of their use" (Suchman 2002: 95) does not work. The discussions about democracy, citizenship and technology in the long run were part of the positive stabilisation, which aimed to situate the often so rhetorical notion of e-democracy in this specific municipality.

---

43   Interview with the project leader on 22 April 2003.

[Christina's Story]

My story is about boundaries, challenges and interventions in computer science (CS) and its knowledge production, with a focus on university education.

I have a background as lecturer in CS. During the late 1990s I worked with a number of projects targeting the situation for the (very few) female students in CS. These projects were no doubt attempts at interventions: interventions into the male dominated culture of computing, interventions in order to support female students and interventions in teaching (an experiment with gender segregated teaching). I would characterise these projects, these interventions, as targeting equality issues, and in fact, creating exclusions instead of inclusions (e.g. singling out female students in the gender segregated teaching project).

During my work with these projects, I gradually started questioning the "women-into-technology"-oriented approaches, realising that the equality project was not enough. I began to think about issues of knowledge within CS. My experience led to my asking other questions, to an interest in the invisible and the taken for granted: the discipline of computer science. At this point I crossed some supposed boundaries into feminist and gender research.

What are the challenging boundaries involved in my work? One of them concerns epistemologies, where the feminist epistemologies that are foundational for me, such as situated knowledge and partial perspectives, are completely different from most of the epistemological foundations of CS. There are also questions of definitions such as what is considered to be CS? These in turn create inclusions and exclusions: who is considered to have valid CS knowledge?

In my intervention, I target questions of integrating feminist research issues into computer science education. What happens when feminist research meets computer science educational practice? I work in a project with CS faculty, where the aim is to bring the participants' practices together with feminist theory and research, in a belief that the latter can shed new and unexpected light on the former. This is accomplished through conversations about knowledge situated in the participants' context, and reflection over their own experience as teachers, with contributions from feminist research. A special focus has been the teaching of programming and the 'paradigms' implicit in this teaching. A goal is to try to make hidden views and expectations visible, and to work to accommodate greater diversity in the practices of CS as well as among its practitioners.

In this intervention project, and in my research as a whole, I find it important to ask questions that are unexpected, surprising, perhaps even provocative. Asking questions can be a way to start a reflective process as well as a way to communicate.

I want to do what could be called feminist computer science research. What is this? Does it exist? Is it even possible? Is it possible to refuse categories and boundaries? I have the (impossible?) intention of being *both* a computer scientist and a feminist researcher. Norwegian informaticians[44] Tone Bratteteig and Guri Verne challenge the existing dichotomies: "We think it is of vital importance to stay an informatician, but with an interest in feminist research, refusing to resolve this dilemma by choosing one of these areas of research. By doing this, we do not accept the dichotomy between feminism and technology. The challenge is to learn to live with, and possibly harvest from, the contradictions and alleged paradoxes that arise." (Bratteteig and Verne 1997: 70).

However, I do not only make interventions into CS as a feminist researcher, I also make interventions as a computer scientist into feminist research. What is permitted among feminist researchers, such as ideas, opinions, writing style, language, etc.? The attempt to be both computer scientist and feminist researcher leads to conflicts, not the least of which are internal, within my person. These conflicts, or tensions, originate to a large extent in the different epistemologies and scientific traditions. To cope with this, I think that the research environment is crucial. It must be acceptable to be both computer scientist and feminist technoscience researcher, and not to have to choose or force one part to adapt to the other, but rather enter into conversations. Thus, I find 'impurity' and inter-/trans-disciplinarity very important. The research within technoscience studies provides space for experimentation and exploration, opening possibilities for new approaches, making it possible to move between positions and see many different images and stories. The result is a more complex understanding, which also allows for translations and transformations.

[Lena's Story]

I want to illustrate why our feminist technoscience research has identified research transformation as the core issue and why I emphasise the transformation 'project' to be directed towards and located within our own knowledge producing body – that is, the technical university itself. One of the necessary prerequisites for research transformation is the development of a broader epistemological infrastructure in places where we conduct academic research, where many have difficulties even with the spelling of the word epistemology. It is not my intention to be ironic here, but to recognise the dominant norms of my own

---

44   "Informatics is the term for computer science departments in universities in Norway, indicating
      that the discipline is defined more broadly than in traditional computer science departments."
      (Bratteteig and Verne 1997: 59)

academic education within faculties of natural science and technology. Becoming an active partner in knowledge production, whether you are a feminist technoscience researcher or not, demands skills also in epistemological reflection and positioning. This means that the way knowledge is understood and produced within the technical spheres is vital for functional and relevant IT development in its specific context.

With a background in natural science, technology and non-formal adult education, my professional life has been characterised by the development of complex understandings about knowledge and research processes within technoscience, with a special focus on IT. Low-income countries and the postcolonial context are important for my work, which also includes techno- and research-political studies. My own experience concerning the motives for transformation is not surprisingly also recognised elsewhere[45]. Developing appropriate and relevant technology solutions is a complex and context-dependent issue and has been developed in many technology fields (see e.g. Rydhagen 2002).

An example of how feminist technoscience is a resource for research transformation is illustrated by a project (see below) involving an integrated regional development process built on applied IT. The project relies on transformation in mindset (and practice) of one of the main actors in the process, namely the university with its research resources. The region in question, Blekinge, situated in the southeast of Sweden, is a region that has undergone tremendous structural change during the 1990s. From dependence on heavy industry and military service the region now focuses on IT development in industry and the educational system with a new technical university (BTH) that has an explicit profile of applied IT. The regional development process implies recognition of techno-politics and research-politics as rooted in an understanding of knowledge and technology production as processes that occur in distributed knowledge systems (Gibbons et al. 1994; Nowotny et al. 2001). In other words, knowledge creation today takes place in the boundary areas between universities, companies (the private sector) and other actors in regional, national and international public sectors. We find these processes also in the Blekinge region and in the research and development carried out at BTH. A linearly focused process must be replaced by an approach characterised by understanding of knowledge and technology as more complex, non-linear processes. It is exactly here we find feminist technoscience to be a resource as it has emphasised research and technology development as complex, context dependent and co-

---

45   The most recent references I would mention here are the numerous documents published within the WSIS (World Summit on Information Society) process, see www.genderwsis.org, www.itu.int/wsis.

evolving activities (se e.g. Wagner 1994; Haraway 1997; Gulbrandsen 2004; Rydhagen 2002; Elovaara 2004; Björkman 2005).

On a more concrete level, the project is situated in the development, since 2000, of a new university campus at BTH. The university is an active, cooperative partner in a local innovation node[46] called NetPort.Karlshamn[47], which envisions becoming a competence centre focusing on technology development within new media, experience-based learning and intelligent transport systems. The other two main partners are local government and industry. One model explored for the processes taking place, in which the three actors mentioned co-operate, has been a triple helix stating that the three institutional bodies – the university, industry and government – are increasingly working together (Johansen and Uhlin 2001). The triple helix model focuses mainly on the outer framework of the co-evolving processes. The actual knowledge and development processes are more explicitly discussed within the concept of "mode 2" (Nowotny et al. 2001). Mode 2 knowledge production is characterised by its:

- situation in the context of application
- emphasis on distributed knowledge processes
- development of robust knowledge
- accountability in multiple contexts.

On a rhetorical level a traditional university can accomplish this understanding. But in practice this is highly challenging because it demands research transformation.

Researchers and teachers at Technoscience studies with its base in feminist technoscience have been deeply involved in the development processes of the distributed knowledge and technology producing system NetPort. For more detailed information about the concrete results of NetPort so far, see Trojer and Henningsson (2005).

The example given illustrates the need for attention to epistemological infrastructure in order to be able to work transformatively within the knowledge and technology producing body (BTH). This work has been identified as one mission for feminist technoscience (Björkman 2005; Trojer 2002; Elovaara 2004).

---

46   A local organisation/system within which several active partners cooperate to create innovations, economical and societal growth.

47   www.netport.karlshamn.se

Discussion

The stories told seem to be quite different from the perspectives of 'what, where and how', but the aim of the activities and processes described is the same: to gain experience in epistemological exercises, where issues of knowledge are central. The three stories show how feminist technoscience can intervene in a variety of arenas, both inside and outside academia. They address what happens when feminist situated epistemologies move to different contexts; what the possibilities and tensions are with respect to cooperation.

Feminist research has for a long time made great efforts to understand and develop the ideas of otherness and difference. Our experience tells us that this discussion is also extremely central and relevant when speaking about the focus of feminist technoscience on IT. What we must do is investigate how questions concerning differences and otherness need to be reformulated and situated in the context of IT. We have seen that the differences present in technoscience/IT practices often show up in tensions concerning issues of epistemology, knowledge production, expertise, participation and implementation, as well as in political and societal development. The world of information technology, as is the case for all other worlds, consists of power-differentiated communities. This differentiation is at the same time an essential part of the different actors' collective dreams of "how things might be different" (Haraway 1991: 93). There is no room for innocence, but at the same time, there is also no place for never-ending conflicts. There should be room for "an earthwide network of connections, including the ability partially to translate knowledges among very different...communities." (Haraway 1991: 187) By recounting our experience, we want to show that this translation work – where there are no ready-made models or methods – is both possible and a very difficult task. We have no illusions that the work can be done immediately, extensively or without collisions.

IT and other technoscience practices are so tightly interwoven with our lives that stepping outside of these to analyse and criticize is not a position available to feminist technoscience research. On the contrary, impure places and actions are the only options we have because we have to participate in situated, concrete practices "...that cobble(s) together non-harmonious agencies and ways of living that are accountable both to their disparate inherited histories and to their barely possible but absolutely necessary joint futures" (Haraway 2003: 7). We would like to end this article by suggesting a list of important challenges, issues and potentials that we see in feminist technoscience research:

- Expand the perceptions of technological knowledge and development.
- Indicate alternative directions of technology/IT applications.

- Make the cultures within technology-related institutions explicitly visible (phase out "the culture of no culture") and thereby show that no research positions are innocent.
- Establish new fora for the development of understandings of the relations between research and politics.
- Act as catalysts for inter- and trans-disciplinary constellations.

This list can be seen as conditions for attempting transformations. But how can we initiate and participate in a movement that aims at trustworthy interventions and processes of change? As the list suggests, the work cannot and ought not to be done by feminist technoscience researchers alone. When one of the fundamental bases for change is to look for and build alliances, we have to learn to cooperate – also with people who do not always share our own epistemological and political concerns. We have to learn to ask new kinds of questions about alliances and collaboration because the alliances and collaboration partners might be in many ways unexpected and strange. The questions are both complicated and absolutely necessary, as Donna Haraway, referring to the work of Helen Verran, writes: "How can people rooted in different knowledge practices 'get together', especially when all-too-easy cultural relativism is not an option, either politically, epistemologically, or morally? How can general knowledge be nurtured in postcolonial worlds [or other worlds – our addition] committed to taking difference seriously?" (Haraway 2003: 7). Taking differences seriously means that there is a need to find a position from which to act, where it is possible to respect differences but not to be satisfied with the relativist thought that 'anything goes'. What is instead needed is a desire to get involved in respectful conversations without losing our own feminist epistemological intervention goals.

References

Björkman, Christina (2005): Crossing Boundaries, Focusing Foundations, Trying Translations: Feminist Technoscience Strategies in Computer Science. Doctoral Dissertation. Karlskrona: Blekinge Institute of Technology.

Bowker, Geoffrey C.; Star, Susan Leigh (1999): Sorting Things Out: Classification and Its Consequences. Cambridge, Mass. and London, England: The MIT Press.

Bratteteig, Tone; Verne, Guri (1997): Feminist, or merely critical? In: Moser, Ingunn; Aas, Gro Hanne (eds): Technology and Democracy: Gender, Technology and Politics in Transition? Oslo: Centre for Technology and Culture, University of Oslo: 59-74.

Elovaara, Pirjo (2004): Angels in Unstable Sociomaterial Relations: Stories of Information Technology. Doctoral Dissertation. Karlskrona: Blekinge Institute of Technology.

Gibbons, Michael; Limoges, Camilla; Nowotny, Helga; Schwartzman, Simon; Scott, Peter; Trow, Martin (1994): The New Production of Knowledge. London: Sage.

Gulbrandsen, Elisabeth (2004): How can universities become more active partners in innovation systems? Lessons from the Nordic countries. In: Gulbrandsen, Elisabeth; Nsengiyumva, Albert; Rydhagen, Birgitta; Trojer Lena: ICT, Innovation Systems and the Role of Universities in Societal Development - A (Post)Colonial Strain? Butare: National University of Rwanda Press.

Göranzon, Bo (1991): The Practical Intellect: Computers and Skills. London: Springer.

Haraway, Donna (1991): Simians, Cyborgs and Women: The Reinvention of Nature. London: Free Association Books.

Haraway, Donna (1997): Modest_Witness@Second_Millenium.FemaleMan©_Meets_ OncoMouse™. Feminism and Technoscience. New York and London: Routledge.

Haraway, Donna (2003): The Companion Species Manifesto: Dogs, People and Significant Otherness. Chicago: Prickly Paradigm Press.

Harding, Sandra (1986): The Science Question in Feminism. Ithaca: Cornell University Press.

Johansen, Ragnar; Uhlin, Åke (2001): Innovation and the Post-academic Condition. The Case of Vestfold University College and the "Electronic Coast" Project. Available http://smealsearch2.psu.edu/134277.html. Accessed 2006-02-17.

Latour, Bruno (1999): Pandora's Hope: Essays on the Reality of Science Studies. Cambridge, Mass. and London, England: Harvard University Press.

Lykke, Nina; Markussen, Randi; Olesen, Finn (2000): There Are Always More Things Going on than You Thought! Methodologies as Thinking Technologies. Interview with Donna Haraway. In: Kvinder, Køn & Forskning 4: 52-60.

Mörtberg, Christina (2003): In Dreams Begins Responsibility – Feminist Alternatives to Technoscience. In: Mörtberg, Christina; Elovaara, Pirjo; Lundgren, Agneta (eds): How do we make a difference? Luleå: Luleå University of Technology: 57-69.

Nowotny, Helga; Scott, Peter; Gibbons, Michael (2001): Rethinking Science: Knowledge and the Public in the Age of Uncertainty. Cambridge: Polity Press.

Regeringen proposition 1995/96: 86 Åtgärder för att öka användning av IT [Government Bill. 1995/96:86 Measures to Broaden and Develop the Use of Information Technology]. Available: http://www.regeringen.se. Accessed 2005-12-12.

Regeringens proposition 1999/2000: 125 Ett informationssamhälle för alla [Government Bill 1999/2000: 125 An Information Society for All]. Available: http://www.regeringen.se. Accessed 2005-12-12.

Rydhagen, Birgitta (2002): Feminist Sanitary Engineering as a Participatory Alternative in South Africa and Sweden. Doctoral Dissertation. Karlskrona: Blekinge Institute of Technology.

Suchman, Lucy (2002): Located Accountabilities in Technology Production. In: Scandinavian Journal of Information Systems 12 (2): 91-105.

Suchman, Lucy; Blomberg, Jeanette; Orr, Julian; Trigg, Randy (1999): Reconstructing Technologies as Social Practice. In: American Behavioral Scientist 43 (3): 392-408.

Trojer, Lena (2002): Genusforskning inom teknikvetenskap – en drivbänk för forskningsförändring [Gender Research within Technoscience – a Hotbed for Research Transformation]. Stockholm: Swedish National Agency for Higher Education.

Trojer, Lena; Henningsson, Samuel (2005): Why Triple Helix? Bulletin of the KPZK 217 (Polish abbreviation of 'Polish National Committee for Space Economy and Regional Planning').

Wagner, Ina (1994): Connecting Communities of Practice: Feminism, Science and Technology. In: Women's Studies International Forum 17 (2/3): 257-265.

III Construction of Information Society Technology

Uncovering the Invisible: Gender-Sensitive Analysis of Call Center Work and Software

Susanne Maass, Els Rommes[48]

"Look at the things that others have forgotten, the things they consider unimportant, the things behind the scenes – and you're likely to find some important deleted work." (Star 1991: 83)

New telecommunication and information technology has enabled a new, booming field of work: customer care in call centers. What are the working conditions of call center employees and does call center technology improve these conditions? To answer these questions, we will combine insights from Applied Computer Science[49], more specifically from the field of participatory design, with insights from social sciences, specifically Gender Studies.

Computer science, in our view, is a discipline that mainly deals with modelling and formalisation (for a more detailed discussion of the image and the practices of CS studies, see Maass, Wiesner 2006). In order to support or automate real world processes, static and dynamic structures in our world first have to be discovered and then explicitly described. One of the main things computer science students are taught is to see structures and to discern recurrent structures in various areas – to see the same in the diverse. They are trained in abstraction and formal description. Hence, in systems analysis computer scientists become quite efficient in seeing similar patterns in what they study and in shielding their perception from what might be particular in the current case. In

48   This chapter contains an analysis of the outcomes of the project ‚Computereinsatz und Arbeitsgestaltung in Call Centern' (computer use and work design in call centers) which was done by Margita Zallmann, Florian Theissing and Susanne Maass. It was financed by the Bremen minister for work, youth, women, health und social affairs and the European Social Fund and was carried out in cooperation with three call centers and the workers board in Bremen. We hereby thank employees and employers of the call centers and the workers board of Bremen for their participation.

49   In Applied Computer Science, the social context of computer design and use is studied (e.g. users, societal effects, desirability of software solutions) with the help of social science methodologies.

a way they standardise what is relevant in the world they model. What does this have to do with gender?

According to perceptual psychology (Neisser 1979) humans first of all perceive those structures that are familiar to them. We primarily see what we know, what we expect and what is important to us. Our life experiences and life situation play an important part in these perceptions. "Our biological sex, whether we are born as male or female, has a large influence on the kinds of experiences we are more likely to have in the course of our life, e.g. on what kinds of toys we are given, whether we give birth or are drafted for the army and how we are perceived and treated by others. These experiences influence our choices, identities and perceptions of ourselves and of the world we live in." (Hagemann-White 1989: 37) Moreover, gender is one of the main ordering structures in society. Our binary understanding of the world as consisting of behaviour, characteristics and items that can be classified as either masculine or feminine influences our perception, which subsequently influences our expectations, behaviour and self-identity. Hence, it is almost unavoidable that computer scientists perceive and model the world along gendered lines and following familiar gender stereotypes, whether or not these stereotypes form an adequate representation of the case being studied.

The outcome of unconsciously gendered design processes may be an inadequate system that does not support the requirements of its users. Especially if designers have been unaware of gender, or gender-blind, they may unconsciously design for the male norm in society, leaving out or making invisible feminine connotated elements of the work or of work done by women in general. This may lead to the system not being used or furthering inequities (Star, Strauss, 1999: 14). The design of the 'smart home' of the future forms a good example. Designers of the 'smart home' have unconsciously modelled their technologies to the male norm of inhabiting houses with priority given to energy saving, safety, communication and entertainment. These features are in general more important to the life and habitation patterns of male inhabitants. Whereas men more often use their house for eating, sleeping and relaxing, for women it is more often a place to work, to socialise and to take care of children. The invisibility of women's habitation patterns in this case may have led to less development of technologies that could be useful for them, such as caring technologies (Berg 1994). Similarly, Wajcman and others have called attention to the fact that suburbs have been called 'sleep villages' by policy-makers, who subsequently based the geographical and mobility-patterns planning on the needs of car-owning, commuting people of whom a large majority was male (Wajcman 1991).

Gender-blind design may also offer an explanation for the 'productivity paradox': the introduction of new technology to increase productivity will actually lead to a drop in productivity because "the invisible work that keeps [socio-technical networks] stabilised will go unaccounted for" (Star 1991: 87). Muller, e.g., found such a productivity paradox in a study on call center agents and explained it by the fact that much of the work of call center agents was ignored by the computer systems meant to support them (Muller 1999: 44). Only after the previously invisible parts of call center agents' work were considered in the software, the anticipated work-time savings were reached.

If, on the other hand, designers are not 'gender blind' but design a new technology based on gender stereotypes, the technology will congeal and reinforce these stereotypes (Rommes 2006). When e.g. computer games for girls are about fashion design for Barbie and are given a pink colour, girls are simultaneously taught to be interested in fashion and to have caring values (while boys are signalled that this is not for boys). Girls with interests other than Barbie are signalled that they do not conform to the female norm. Although some girls, at some point in their lives, like to play with Barbies, design based on stereotypes means that no critical reflection has taken place as to the needs of the particular users of the technology under development, nor about the kind of world we would like to live in. Computer systems design is no 'innocent' activity, as design processes are both shaped by gendered assumptions and perceptions and shape society and the gender-relations therein.

A gender-sensitive look at the social context of software development and use may reveal the gender-biased understandings, priorities and exclusions within the development process. It provides a more diverse picture as a basis for technical innovation than 'normal' software design. In this chapter, we will analyse the work practices of call center employees from a gender-aware perspective and find out to what extent the software that is meant to support them does so adequately, and whether it reinforces gender stereotypes or not. First, we will look at the working conditions of call center employees, and then at the information technologies they use. We will conclude by more generally characterising this approach of gender studies in Applied Computer Science and by suggesting more gender-sensitive methodologies for the early analytic phases of software development.

1   Call Center Work: What Analysis Methods Reveal

The spectrum of call center (CC) services is extremely wide and services cover a wide variety of products. In call center work, a division is made between inbound and outbound services. Hotline agents deal with inbound calls and may offer information or advice on e.g. insurances or technical devices. Similarly, telesales agents respond to inbound calls by taking orders for goods or reservations. Alternatively, telemarketeers make outbound phone calls, e.g. they may dial up potential customers such as all cafés in a certain area and offer demonstration and free use of new coffee machine models. They then arrange dates for their field service personnel. Call centers are organised as internal business units or as independent companies providing services to other companies. In our research project we have studied call center work and software of three call centers of different kinds.

Call center work has all attributes of so-called 'female jobs': the work is considered to be intellectually simple and repetitive, clean and physically light, not technical but rather social – or at least so it seems. Alluding to female stereotypes and life situations, job offers for call center agents implicitly address women: a telemarketing job for a coffee company is announced by "Feel like coffee and communication?" Another ad says "If you are diligent, single-minded and feel like earning money, and if you can smile with your voice you can start immediately." No formal training seems to be required for such jobs. Ads and qualification criteria do not address people seeking a steep and profitable career path. This, too, associates call center work with female employees. CC agents have a low social prestige, get low salaries, have few career options and often work part time. Part time work again ties CC work to 'female work', as in present western society more women than men take the responsibility for caring for children, hence they experience a bigger need for the personal flexibility that part time work seems to offer. In fact, about two thirds of call center agents in Germany were and still are female (cf. Schietinger, Schroth 2001).

To study the requirements and conditions of CC work and to see the extent to which it does indeed follow these (gendered) stereotypes of simple and light work, we have held twelve observational interviews with agents. We followed the principles of ethnographical critical analysis, which state that the researcher has to be present in the context to develop a thorough understanding of the work being done by employees. Moreover, a relationship between researcher and employee needs to be established based on a partnership in which the employee is considered the "master" who teaches the researcher as an "apprentice" about their work. Interpretations of the analysis need to stay as close as possible to what the employees have stated and need to be checked with them. The last but not least of the principles of ethnographical critical analysis is that although the focus of the analysis needs to be clear beforehand, it also needs to be flexible, leaving room for adaptations if other problems or focus points turn out to be more important. (For a detailed description of "contextual interviews" see Beyer, Holtzblatt 1998.)

Our focus of analysis was on the criteria for "humane work" as defined by the "Kontrastive Aufgabenanalyse" KABA (contrastive task analysis method, Dunckel et al. 1993). According to work psychology in general, in order to be considered as humane, work has to require a wide variety of personal competencies and to allow for further development of these competencies. KABA characterises humane work by great latitudes regarding responsibilities ("decision latitude"), temporal planning and cooperation with others; also by variety in task aspects, transparency of and influence on working procedures and a low degree of stress. To comply with the last criterion of critical analysis mentioned above, we remained flexible in our use of the focus of KABA. Hence, when we found out that one of the main factors in the work of call center agents could not be measured with the help of KABA, we have critically analyzed and adapted these criteria. Moreover, we have paid particular attention to those aspects of work that tend to be overseen when focussing on the male norms of what 'work' implies.

So what does a call center agent do? Basically we found that she has to mediate between the requirements her organisation poses to her and the demands of her customers. The organisations CC agents work for want their agents to quickly get the customers' data and initiate some transactions. They define rather strict standards for the interaction with the customer; they decide what products and services agents can offer to whom and how to proceed in the interaction process to be as efficient as possible. Companies define rather short average call times and find ways to display waiting queues to the agents. To handle large numbers of calls, agents are expected to apply strategies to take the lead in conversations and speed up the process. The software they use takes the data input and displays information about and for the customer. Altogether, this results in a general view of well-organised data processing work on a production line. It differs a lot from clerical work where the desk workers can to a certain extent choose in what order to deal with their tasks.

However, in our view, agents' interactive service work requires much flexibility as they face customers who want individual service. An agent will try to somehow compensate for organisational and technical rigidities and deficiencies that result from the production-like organisation of work. At times she will take the risk of disregarding organisational directions in the interest of good customer service. Customers expect friendly and flexible responses to their often unclear and changing wishes. Agents and customers permanently have to cooperate and adjust on a functional and a social level. The interaction process very much depends on the customer. Some callers are well organised and know exactly what they want; some are not cooperative, they may be in a hurry or call from noisy environments. Others take their time to decide and re-decide or just love to talk. This makes the work process very unpredictable for the agent who has to react flexibly and immediately in any situation. If she realises that the customer has no time she may shorten or skip certain phases of the interaction process. If the customer desires something that the software does not easily support she may note customer data on paper and correct the data in the system after the end of the conversation. She may explain at length or look for more information and call back to satisfy customer requests. Thus, agents as intermediaries balance the partly conflicting interests of their organisation and their customers.

In the course of our analyses in the workplace we realised that the criteria of the well established task analysis method KABA we were using could not sufficiently characterise the tasks we studied. The criterion "decision latitude" discriminates task requirements only on the functional level. In most cases of CC work the decision latitude is rather low: agents have no choice to sell products cheaper or refuse to answer a question. Such decisions have been taken by the organisation itself - agents just carry out what they are advised to do. However, on the social level where "emotion work" (Hochschild 2003) is being done, they very often develop strategies and take decisions themselves. They take responsibility for how to display emotions in order to influence the customer's emotions. To describe the options agents have to act on the level of communication, we introduced a new criterion we called "interaction latitude". (For more detail see Theissing, Maass 2006.) So while their behaviour in customer interaction may seem predefined and not very challenging (low functional decision latitude), their tasks may in fact be quite demanding and rich on the social level. Similarly, another study of CC work arrived at the conclusion that CC work is much more complicated than generally is thought as it contains "significant aspects of expertise and knowledge work" (Muller 1999: 36). According to Muller, developers, human-computer interaction experts and vendors of software systems had not seen the complicated aspects of CC work, amongst other reasons because of gender biases in analytic techniques. Our new criterion allows us to see and characterise this additional interaction latitude that may organisationally and technologically be more or less granted and supported.

Most of today's task analysis methods primarily aim at production work and clerical work rather than at work where interaction is of primary importance. Researchers and practitioners in work psychology must be asked why there are almost no adequate analysis instruments for person-oriented service work. Could it be the case that the requirements of such fields that count as female (let alone house and family work) remain invisible or less relevant to them, as has often been pointed out by gender researchers (Smith 1987)?

Our research helped to deconstruct the image of simple and unqualified CC service work and showed how complicated their work really was. In line with this finding, another study on call center agents in Bremen revealed that in fact their general level of education was very high: more than 20% had graduated from secondary school (Abitur), more than 60% had finished vocational training and 7% even had a university degree (Baumeister 2001). Similarly, the high percentage of part time positions may not reflect the wish of (female) call center agents to combine their work with family obligations, but rather the fact that part time positions were organisationally desirable from the standpoint of personnel planning in accordance to variable service demands. This requires a high degree of flexibility on the part of the employees. Moreover, the high level of part time work amongst CC agents reflects the fact that interactive service work on the phone is physically and mentally very strenuous; it requires almost permanent concentration and often cannot be done for 8 hours a day. The image of call center work as 'simple' work certainly does not fit. Our next question is to what extent the software used by call center agents supported the multiple facets of CC agents' work.

2   Evaluating Software for Interactive Service Work

Call center agents work with various sorts of software. In fact, the whole idea of efficient centralised customer service via call centers depends on computer technology. Automatic call distribution systems (ACD) manage incoming calls and direct them to "the next available agent". Computer-telephone integration allows to identify a calling customer and to display her data immediately for the agent receiving her call. Customer relationship management systems store and process customer, product and transaction data, keeping and disclosing the customer contact history for any agent dealing with that customer at any time. Automatic diallers speed up the dialling process for outbound calls and interactive dialogue scripts steer the agent along the standard phases of customer interaction. Does this software support all the facets of their work as we analysed above, or was it rather based on gendered stereotypes of call center work as being simple, repetitive work strictly following routines? In other words, does it confirm and reinforce gender stereotypes on what female work means, or is it designed on the basis of what call center agents point out as relevant in practice?

In tests with users and in expert reviews we evaluated the agents' software for its usability and probed for task adequacy and deficiencies. Following a participatory approach, we cooperated with the agents, taking care to include as many women as possible. In one of the CC we studied, software was to support the processes in which callers would order electronic parts or inquire their price and get advice about their properties or about equivalent products. Products and written offers would then be sent to them by mail. Figure 1 shows the steps the CC agents and their customers have to take to accomplish this process. First the customer identifies herself (1). The existing customer data such as address, contact person and paying modality, are quickly verified and updated (2). Then she chooses to either order parts or get a price offer (3). Product data are typed in (4) and the transaction is terminated (5). This triggers a shipping process. Obviously this software models customer interaction as a highly structured information exchange that follows a clear and uniform logic. In order to achieve efficiency, such software is optimised with respect to data transfer rates, parallel display of customer and product data and the sequence of transactions according to an ideal one-best-way customer dialog.

However, as we have shown in the analysis of CC agents' work, customer interaction does not always take this ideal course. Callers with just a short question refuse to identify themselves. Others first want to check whether the desired product is in stock, before they are ready to discuss paying modalities. Very often a caller changes her mind in the middle of the conversation; she only orders some of the parts and wants a price offer for the rest. Since the software requires an early decision (order or offer?), agents must find work-arounds and explain and compensate software rigidity on a communication and emotional level. Clearly, the designers did not see how crucial flexibility in interaction is to be able to offer service of a high quality. Rigid software that neglects the actual complexity and diversity of dialogues impairs flexible customer service. Hence, rather than supporting their work, in this respect CC technology posed an extra burden on the agents.

Based on our task analyses and the subsequent software evaluations we came to the conclusion that CC software was designed on the basis of the stereotypes of simple female work rather than to fit customer interaction as we have learned to see it. Careful analysis of CC agents' tasks and usability tests of CC software showed many software deficiencies, in particular lacking task-adequacy and a lack of support for social, interactive and emotional aspects of CC agents' work. One could argue that only a limited or restricted understanding of work-processes can be incorporated in software design anyway, following the inherent modelling and formalisation requirements. However, for one of our partner companies we developed our assessment further into a prototype for a new interface to the front office systems used in customer interaction, showing that an alternative design in fact was possible. In our software revision with the agents we made an effort to design it task-adequate with respect to the social aspects of interaction. This "interaction adequacy" first of all requires efficient input and high flexibility regarding the sequence of transactions. Standard proceedings may be implemented, but a deviation without loss must always be possible. The agent must be supported in keeping an overview and remaining in control of the interaction process. (For more detail see Maass et al. 2002.) The revised software that later was developed from our prototype was well received and very much appreciated by the agents.

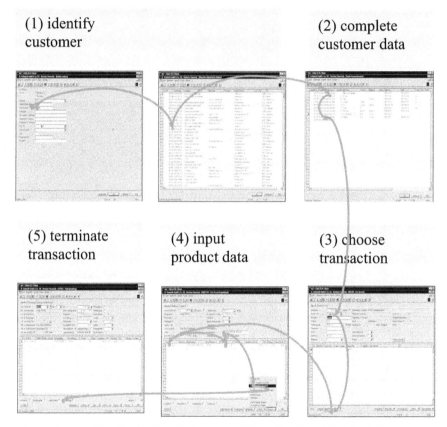

(1) identify customer

(2) complete customer data

(5) terminate transaction

(4) input product data

(3) choose transaction

Figure 1:   One-Best-Way of Customer Interaction (with Click Trail)

It seems that earlier developers of the software had overlooked or ignored the complicatedness of the work done by call center agents. Hence, they had tried to capture and standardise parts of the work that were too complicated to be formalised and standardised. Call center agents needed their software to support their interaction latitude rather than ignore this part of their work. In addition to developing software that was more supportive to the call center agents than the previous one, our detailed report on agents' tasks, their strategies and know-how, their situation in customer interaction, and their obvious commitment to good customer service had the advantage of making those parts of their work visible that had previously been ignored. Indeed, our report was received with surprise by management and technical staff. It seemed that for the first time management and IT experts got a lively impression of CC agents' work. They learned what CC service demands from the agents and what the effects of software are that is not optimised for interactive work. The agents, on their part, learned that software does not have to be accepted as it is and that they themselves have the know-how to stand up for and inform software revision. So, for those agents involved, our project lead to an increase of knowledge, of professional self-esteem and to a sense of empowerment.

3   Conclusions

It is striking that the designers of the CC software as well as of scientific work analysis instruments such as KABA oversaw particularly those aspects of service work that the agents themselves described as extremely relevant for good service: flexible communication and emotion work. And exactly those aspects of the job have a feminine connotation. According to Muller, "historically, the culture and work of people marked as different from the main-stream has been analyzed as simple or even inferior" (Muller 1999: 51), in this case they were even not seen at all. Indeed, in call center work, service mentality and com-munication skills were not considered professional abilities that must be acquired, as the mentioned advertisements showed. Rather they are assumed to be something women have 'by nature' and as such can be taken for granted. For CC agents the necessary professional skills shrink to "the smile in their voice".

The stereotypic connection of social and interaction skills with femininity and with 'natural' skills that can be observed here may also be responsible for the low validation, wages and appreciation for this kind of work. Indeed, as has been shown in many previous studies, feminisation is known to 'devaluate' professional fields. Not seeing undervalued or invisible female work may mean that such work is not rewarded. Work aspects that remain invisible will not be included in the model of work that forms the fundament for the development of technologies that are supposed to support workers. Hence, we can conclude that the designers of the CC software were 'gender blind'. This may lead, as Star and

Strauss would argue, to "more 'shadow work' or invisible work (...) as well as the (sometimes) obvious social justice and inequity issues" (Star, Strauss 1999: 20). In the case we studied, ignoring the interaction latitude part of the call center work in the software system meant that agents spent more time to work around the software system in order to maintain the level of service and interaction latitude they wanted to offer: a good example of the productivity paradox.

To summarise, our gender-sensitive view on interactive service work in CC has in fact revealed gender biased understandings, priorities and valuations of call center work that are mirrored, congealed and reinforced by technology. Gender studies stress the importance of being aware of how power is divided and to look for the invisible and the undervalued. From there on, we can start looking for ways to overcome power-imbalances. In our case participatory methods have been shown to serve to empower those who normally have no say in analysis and design and who have to work with technology as the experts have conceived it for them. We have also shown how the perspective of gender studies and especially their focus on stereotypes and the invisible and undervalued aspects of what counts as feminine may help to improve participatory analysis and design. We have uncovered hidden aspects of CC work, consequently we can offer a new concept (interaction adequacy) for the scientific discussion of work-oriented software design and an additional criterion (interaction latitude) to append to the KABA criteria of humane work.[50]

The detailed account of our CC study was meant to show that Applied Computer Science and Gender Studies can be combined successfully. Applied CS projects offer opportunities for Gender Studies to enter and influence the field of technology construction or more generally, the field of technological innovation. By entering this field, not only an analysis or deconstruction is possible, but also suggestions for (re)construction can be made. Likewise the gender perspective may serve as an eye-opener in the field of technology development and critique. Exemplarily it points out social differences, reveals mistaken generalisations and highlights power structures in society. It helps to study application areas and leads to a refined understanding of the diverse requirements of institutions and people: employees, customers and other persons affected by new software. It serves to anticipate and interpret effects of new technology and to assess and refine the methods applied in technology construction. Combining the two may eventually lead to a world in which invisibility and undervaluation of work and people is no longer gendered.

---

50 Like Muller, we discovered "important relationships between choice of analytic technique and visibility of operators' work": (....) "invisible work is invisible to someone or from a particular perspective" (Muller 1999: 34, 31).

108   Susanne Maass, Els Rommes

References

Berg, Ann-Jorunn (1994): A gendered socio-technical construction: the smart house. In: Cockburn, Cynthia; Furst-Dilic, Ruza (eds.): Bringing technology home. Gender and technology in a changing Europe. Buckingham: Open University Press: 165-180.

Baumeister, Hella (2001): Call Center in Bremen. Strukturen, Qualifikationsanforderungen und Entwicklungstendenzen. Bremen: Arbeitnehmerkammer.

Beyer, Hugh B.; Holtzblatt, Karen (1998): Contextual Design. Defining Customer-Centered Systems. San Francisco: Morgan Kaufmann.

Dunckel, Heiner; Volpert, Walter; Zölch, Martina; Kreutner, Ulla; Pleiss, Cordula; Hennes, Karin (1993): Kontrastive Aufgabenanalyse im Büro – Der KABA-Leitfaden. Grundlagen und Manual. Zürich/Stuttgart: Verlag der Fachvereine/Teubner.

Hagemann-White, Carol (1989). Geslacht en gedrag (F. d. Boer, Trans.). In: Sevenhuijsen, Selma; Outshoorn, Joyce (eds.): Socialisties-Feministiese Teksten 11. Baarn: Ambo: 33-48.

Hochschild, Arlie Russell (2003): The Managed Heart. Commercialization of Human Feeling. University of California Press.

Maass, Susanne; Wiesner, Heike (2006): Programmieren, Mathe und ein bisschen Hardware ... Wen lockt dies Bild der Informatik? In: Informatik Spektrum, 29 (2): 125-132.

Maass, Susanne; Theissing, Florian; Zallmann, Margita (2002): Unterstützung von Interaktionsarbeit im Call-Center. Neue Fragen für die arbeitsorientierte Softwareentwicklung. In: i-com. Zeitschrift für interaktive und kooperative Medien, 2002 (3): 4-11.

Muller, Michael J. (1999): Invisible Work of Telephone Operators: An Ethnocritical Analysis. In: Computer Supported Cooperative Work 8: 31-61.

Neisser, Ulric (1979): Kognition und Wirklichkeit. Prinzipien und Implikationen der kognitiven Psychologie. Stuttgart: Klett-Cotta

Rommes, Els (2006): Gender sensitive design practices. In: Trauth, Eileen M. (ed.): Encyclopedia of Gender and Information Technology. Hershey, Penns.: Idea Group: 675-681

Schietinger, Marc; Schroth, Jochen (2001): Auswertung der Beschäftigtenstruktur in Call Centern. Arbeitspapier 2001-02 Forschungsprojekt Personalmanagement - Call Center und Handel (FREQUENZ). Gelsenkirchen: Institut Arbeit und Technik.

Smith, Dorothy E. (1987): The Everyday World as Problematic. A Feminist Sociology. Stratford: Open University Press/Milton Keynes.

Star, Susan Leigh (ed.) (1991): Invisible Work and Silenced Dialogues in Knowledge Representation. Amsterdam: Elsevier Science.

Star, Susan Leigh; Strauss, Anselm (1999): Layers of Silence, Arenas of Voice: The Ecology of Visible and Invisible Work. In: Computer Supported Cooperative Work 8: 9-30.

Theissing, Florian; Maass, Susanne (2006): KABA im Call-Center. In: Dunckel, Heiner; Pleiss, Cordula (eds.): Leitfaden zur Kontrastiven Aufgabenanalyse. 2nd revised edition. Zürich: Verlag der Fachvereine: 161-179.

Wajcman, Judy (1991): Feminism confronts technology. Cambridge: Polity Press.

E-Empowerment of Heterogeneous Feminist Networks

Tanja Carstensen, Gabriele Winker

From its beginning, the Internet has prompted euphoric hopes for strengthening the women's movement, more gender equality, new public spaces for feminist issues and world wide networking, solidarity and community building of women. In our research project "E-Empowerment. The Use of the Internet in Women's Political Networks", we reviewed these euphoric prognoses and confronted them with empirically founded findings. We examined whether it is possible for feminist networks to increase their influence and power via the Internet (Schachtner, Winker 2005). In the context of this research project it was not possible to simply enquire into the impact of the Internet on feminist politics, because this question suggests that the Internet is a stable, fixed technology with definite effects. Instead, the Internet is in a permanent state of change and can be designed by different actors.

In order to avoid one-sided analyses of the relation between technology and gender that harbour a tendency towards technological determinism, the sociology of technology has developed different theories and perspectives over the last decades. In this article, we therefore outline the sociological debate on technology and apply it to the Internet. Further, we present the results of our research project and consider the complex interaction and the problems between feminist networks and the Internet in terms of the sociology of technology. Following this, we discuss a specific further development of the Internet as an idea to increase the possibilities for empowerment of feminist networks.

1   From Determining Artefacts to Interacting Actants

Since the 1980s, it has been widely accepted within the sociology of technology that technology is socially constructed, formed and negotiated. According to this understanding, technological artefacts are not only open to differing ways of use; their technical construction is also not limited to a single correct form. Technology offers "interpretative flexibility" and is open to social influences.

These insights from Science and Technology Studies (STS) and the Social
Construction of Technology approach (SCOT) focus research attention on the
processes of negotiation and conflicts surrounding the production and use of
technological artefacts, and negate the previously dominant deterministic
approaches to technology (Bijker et al. 1987; MacKenzie, Wajcman 1999).

At the same time, the emphasis on societal influence and formation of
technology has led scholars to neglect the "active" role and powerful effect of
technology. Technological artefacts certainly do have an effect on everyday life.
Social constructivist approaches are therefore now regarded as too unbalanced or
reductionist (Singer 2003: 111). Scholars generally agree that technology and
society mutually constitute or co-construct each other (Wajcman 2004: 106).
This approach admits that technology, despite its interpretative flexibility and
constructed character, also plays an important role in the constitution and
construction of society. So, if we analyze technology, we have to consider both,
the role of societal influences on shaping technology and the active role of
technology changing society.

In analogy to Judith Butler's (1993) concept of the materialisation of
bodies, Winker (2005a) develops the idea of co-materialisation, that is the
simultaneous formation of technological artefacts and human bodies. According
to this concept, human and non-human entities, as described by Haraway (1991:
197ff), or "actants", as Latour (1996) calls human and non-human agents[51], are
produced by linguistic discourses and practices of action. Neither one nor the
other exists previously. That is, neither the human actors have a unilateral
influence on the technological artefacts, nor do the technological artefacts have a
unilateral influence on the human actors. Rather, they are all co-players and
opponents in various games (Singer 2003: 119). The materialised artefacts also
"speak", they matter and restrict or extend the scope of other co-players' options.
However, not all actants may be regarded as of equal status, but join in the game
with differing incorporated power.

In this understanding, things also "do politics" and are not just passive
objects in societal changes. Donna Haraway (1991: 153) understands human and
non-human entities as stakeholders in the political arena. Machines, institutions,
organisms, etc. are capable of action and do intervene. Due to their materiality,
objects and bodies become active stakeholders; they raise problems and make
demands. Thus, they also decide over influence and power relationships.
However, these interventions must not be thought of as intentional. The political
potential of materiality does not lie in putting intentions into practice. Instead, it

51   An actant is "something that acts or to which activity is granted by others" (Latour 1996: 373).
      Human and non-human entities act as actants in heterogeneous networks.

lies in shifting the power-laden structures in which various stakeholders in political processes "interact" (Straube 2004: 134f).

Interestingly however, the Internet research that has arisen over the past few years has fallen back behind these achievements of sociological technology studies and has taken less notice of their discussions. Whereas one-sided questions of the effects and consequences of technology had become increasingly irrelevant within the sociology of technology, they are experiencing a remarkable comeback with regard to the Internet (cf. Carstensen 2005: 65, 228). The majority of Internet studies concentrate firstly on the use of the Internet by individuals, and secondly on the effects of the Internet on these individuals (cf. Paulitz 2005: 11). In such studies, the Internet is frequently assumed to be a more or less given and complete artefact, available and ready for use and with clear effects. The feminist debates around democratisation and empowerment also harbour explanation patterns tending towards technological determinism in many cases (cf. Drüeke, Winker 2005), which attribute emancipatory effects to the Internet per se. What is missing is, on the one hand, a more social constructivist view on the Internet and, on the other hand, approaches that consider the Internet, its "constructors" and its "users" as interacting actants where none of them has a unilateral influence on the other.

2   E-Empowerment in German Feminist Networks

Corresponding to the idea of co-materialisation, we must consider the societal *and* the technological stakeholders for questions of women's empowerment[52] and strengthening feminist politics. This entails examining how feminist actors construct and use the Internet on the one hand, how the Internet actively intervenes and restricts or extends the scope of possibilities on the other hand, and thus how they interact as co-players and opponents within societal power relations. In the context of our research project, we have attempted to investigate the complex relation between feminist actors and technological artefacts in this way. To make the interactions between social actors and technological artefacts clear, we will start by outlining the current situation of feminist networks and then describe their use and design of the Internet. Following on from this, we

---

52   The term empowerment, first coined by Rappaport (1984), is closely linked to the US civil and women's rights movements. Through cooperation, people in marginal positions can use and develop their own sources of power to gain greater self-determination and control over their own lives. Simultaneously, empowerment also refers to collective political self-organization, enabling disadvantaged sections of the population to articulate their interests, participate in political processes and gain power. The concept of empowerment not only criticizes existing power relationships, but also demonstrates perspectives for change.

will explain how the Internet and the feminist activists act together as actants in heterogeneous networks and permanently co-materialise each other.

2.1 Contemporary Challenges for Feminist Networks

The women's movement is currently facing several new challenges. Various societal and political changes are behind this:

In the 1970s, activists accepted the discrimination of women as a whole as a fact, and it was only a question of the correct political emancipation strategy – equality feminism versus difference feminism. From the mid-1980s, however, the focus shifted to take account of the differences between women. Since the mid-1990s, under the influence of postmodernist theories and the reception of the work of Judith Butler (1990), a sceptical attitude towards group identities has been becoming increasingly influential. These are seen as repressive and creating exclusion. The accompanying demand to involve further dimensions of differentiation alongside gender, such as class, ethnicity and sexuality, has led to important new insights. However, it has also made it more difficult to justify and realize feminist activities.

Furthermore, in the Western industrialised nations, an increasing number of women are being integrated into the labour market, the education level of young women and men has reached an equal level to a major extent, and lifestyles are becoming increasingly pluralized. Young women take the existence of equality for granted. In the context of a broad process of state deregulation, feminist projects that see their responsibility as supporting socially disadvantaged groups are losing their financial means, often with the justification that equal opportunities have allegedly been achieved. At the same time, however, single parents, returners to work, women with low formal qualification levels or migrant women, for example, are subject to intensified discrimination processes.

These changes have led to unease and uncertainty among those interested in feminist politics. The subject of women's movements is becoming more difficult to define. Simultaneously, the projects and networks are suffering funding cuts and closures. In everyday life for feminist activists, the burden of work and pressure of costs and time are on the increase. (Winker 2005b)

2.2 Using and Designing the Internet for Feminist Politics

In order to study how feminist networks use and design the Internet in this situation and how the Internet simultaneously intervenes in feminist activity, we worked with various research methods: we evaluated the Internet presences of 200 German women's networks, held 20 interviews with feminist activists on their use of the Internet, and recorded users' search strategies and thereby the possibilities of finding feminist content on the Internet. We also held workshops with women users and an online future workshop with female Internet experts, to develop wishes and suggestions for improvement.

The findings of these steps make up a relatively clear picture: the politically active women use the Internet primarily for finding and providing information. The feminist networks present a wide variety of information regarding their work on their websites, along with specialised information, dates of events, link lists and much more. Thus, the networks involved in the study design and construct the Internet as an information tool. Equally, from the users' point of view, searching for information is the most important use of the Internet. The women we interviewed stated that they use the Internet to clarify organisational questions, and to find information on current political debates or on their working area. The possibilities of accessing important information quickly and easily and making information publicly available are perceived as central advantages of the Internet. According to the interviewees, however, the flood of information and the fact that the net is not organised are negative and annoying. Our protocols of search situations also show how complicated and unsuccessful searches for feminist information in the unstructured WWW can be. The more open the question or purpose is, the broader, more arbitrary and confusing the search results turn out.

Communication via the Internet takes place almost exclusively via e-mail. The networks themselves neither offer interactive options such as forums and chats particularly frequently, nor do the interviewed women use other forums and chats regularly. The reasons for this non-use stated by the women were that they did not have enough time and that they could not see the benefit of forums and chats. Finally, political actions such as e-mail signature lists or options for online voting virtually never take place in the German feminist context we investigated (see also Carstensen, Winker 2005a).

2.3 Internet and Feminist Networks As Actants

If we now consider these findings as processes of co-construction and co-materialisation, it becomes clear in which way human actants – in this case active feminists – and non-human actants – here diverse Internet functions – interact in heterogeneous networks. One can find actors who design complicated websites in cooperation with diverse Internet software actants. One finds Internet technologies as actants, in the formation of which new requirements and roles arise for feminist activists. Examples are mailing lists, which create a flow of information and stress through their daily mail deliveries, or e-mail enquiries, which have to be answered. One finds arbitrarily structured link lists alongside structured databases, links that go nowhere and interrupt search alongside links that lead to good results. Permanently produced and rejected hit lists from search engines, arising from connections between certain keyword combinations and complex technological functions, are the joint result of human and non-human actions.

On the one hand, the activists themselves are involved in constructing the Internet, producing it by building websites and filling them with information, posting on mailing lists and setting up moderated chats. They create links, network sites or let forums slowly die. Feminists intervene and design the Internet according to their requirements. On the other hand, feminist users are confronted, as co-players, with few possibilities to find feminist information, well or poorly sorted link lists, abandoned forums, etc. These actants intervene in the users' everyday political lives and make demands of them. The Internet makes its own contribution, with a new public sphere in which one has to be present, information that has to be managed and communicative possibilities that encourage exchanges of opinions.

The Internet and the feminist networks materialise themselves anew every day as heterogeneous social and technological networks, and this process promotes their further development. But what do these findings imply for the question of an empowerment of women via the Internet? How can empowerment be improved from this perspective?

3   From Platforms to Neighbourhoods

It would be wrong to conclude that feminist networks do not make sufficient use of the existing possibilities of the Internet for strengthening their concerns or that it would be good if they made more use of them. We propose not to take the Internet as a given, though certainly influential entity, but also as incomplete, open to interpretation and change. So how can the networks of Internet and feminist actors work and act jointly to shift power structures and empower themselves?

The results of the interviews, the workshops and the software protocols of the Internet search strategies show that the Internet presents itself most reluctantly in feminist everyday life, with the huge amount of information it offers. Most of the feminists we investigated are dissatisfied with the confusing character of the information, the lack of structure on the net, the "information trash" and the disconnectedness of similar information. The interviewees and participants felt that Internet searches take up too much time and energy. The protocols of Internet searches also show how much effort it is for users to have to gather information on a single subject from the farthest reaches of the Internet. This "information chaos" disrupts and burdens feminist work. One interviewee formulated the problem as follows (our translation):

"I often find searching hard work, and you don't always find what you'd hoped for. I do think that there should perhaps be even (...) more pointers or better structure. At the moment it's just a complete mess and, well, sometimes you get a hit straight away, that's great, but sometimes, if you're searching with combinations, (...) you still have huge numbers of sites but not exactly what you want, so sites you have to go into first and then you realise: but that's not at all what I wanted."

According to the interviewees, the most important concern is the wish for structure, concentration and pre-filtering of the available information. They also wanted information to be easier to find. Several interviewees formulated the idea of an "entry portal":

"...where you really get an overview, what areas there are, and where you know, gosh, there's a starting point, and then from there I can look further (...). Like a kind of sorting, I think, would be just great. So that you always really look for something specific. Just have a kind of access point to start with. (...) it doesn't have to be one starting point, but maybe two or three. (...) And maybe search, where there are things on offer, how could you summarise them."

This prompted us to start thinking about ways of structuring and concentrating the existing information. Providing and searching for information is the main concern of the interviewees and the workshop participants. As they perceive the access to information as a strategically important resource, it appeared crucial for us to take this dissatisfaction as a starting point for looking for design ideas. Thus, we developed the idea of a virtual structuring and linking of the existing information and interaction services in a platform for feminist projects, with the purpose of enabling fast and simple ways to find information relevant for feminists.

Our first step was to develop a database for this purpose, containing the 200 women's networks involved in the study.[53] The feminist networks were initially keyworded according to subject groups (work & career, education & science, or

---

53   see www.frauenbewegung-online.de

violence). This enables users to carry out targeted searches for feminist networks working on a particular subject. Also the features of the networks' websites were registered and entered into the database. This was carried out separately according to the criteria of information, interaction and political action. The information criterion includes link lists, specialised information, job offers, events, etc. The interaction aspect is differentiated between chats, forums, mailing lists, guest books, etc. In this way, it is possible to make a targeted selection from the 200 feminist networks of those that feature a chat room on their site for example, or those that work on the subject of girls and offer a link list on their sites. The software protocols of Internet search strategies we recorded during our project especially show that it is often extremely difficult to search for interactive options such as forums or chats in particular via a normal full-text search (see Carstensen, Winker 2005b: 103f).

The database thus represents an initial attempt to construct a starting point for feminist information on the Internet. It offers search functions beyond the full-text search of a normal search engine. In addition, there is a full-text search option as with a search engine; however this is limited to the 200 evaluated networks. Thus, users can search the full text within a particular – feminist – context. This can focus the search.

However, this form of concentrating and structuring existing feminist websites on the Internet entails new problems. Firstly, such a project is very time-and cost-intensive. Thus, the question arises as to who maintains the database. This extra task is too much for the individual networks, as their resources are already stretched enough. The question regarding a central administration instance is who would finance such an organisation? Secondly, in the case of a centralised coordination, the problem of inclusion and exclusion arises. Should this administrative instance be able to decide who is accepted and who is excluded? Such a procedure is extremely problematical, not only in the light of recent feminist discussions on the differences among women and issues such as transgender. Who is to decide what counts as feminist and what does not? Databases always require a position, whether a group defines itself as a feminist network or not. They always require categorisations, thereby promoting standardisations and exclusions. A key criticism therefore is that this platform may gather networks under one roof that do not wish to have anything to do with each other. Thus, a central platform prompts new problems as a participating actant.

A further development of the database is the concept of Virtual Neighbourhoods (Taube, Winker 2005). Virtual neighbourhood means a cooperation of all interested feminist networks, based on the database. Networks can register for the database and categorise their websites by keywords from a unified problem-specific thesaurus. In a moderated newsgroup belonging to the virtual neighbourhood, the involved networks can discuss the structure of the database and the thesaurus. The newsgroup moderator changes the structure of the database or the thesaurus according to the decisions taken in newsgroup discussions. Thus, there is more self-organisation than in a central platform.

Virtual neighbourhoods also offer new types of search functions that use the thesaurus, and a visualisation of content-related, regional or other relationships. This helps to find a variety of information in a fast and effective way. In addition, a crawler collects all links contained in the websites of the networks in the database. This information is visualised as a graph in order to show the mutual connections within a virtual neighbourhood. This visualisation mirrors the vicinity or distance between the networks, so the problem of gathering very diverse networks under one roof can be partially defused. The networks can position themselves close to other networks via their connecting links, just as they would position themselves in "real life".

Figure 1:   Model of a graphic search option via hypertree,
                 Source: Taube, Winker (2005: 118)

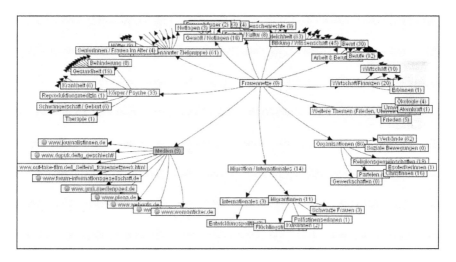

Furthermore, external links to other virtual neighbourhoods could illustrate that being a feminist network is not their only identity and affiliation. A virtual neighbourhood can be thought of as open to all sides. "Feminist network" can then be one category to which a network allocates itself; at the same time, its identity as "gay network", "church network", "academic network" or a self-definition as a "transgender network" can be expressed. Ideas in this direction are certainly very promising for further attempts at structuring content on the Internet and taking the critique of group identities seriously at the same time.

4   Conclusions

Our aim with this article was to develop a perspective of the empowerment of feminist networks via the Internet, in which the Internet is understood as socially constructed and changeable, but which simultaneously takes the "activities" of technology seriously. We wanted to thereby connect the results of feminist Internet research to current debates within the sociology of technology. The idea of various human and non-human co-players equipped with differing resources opened up an image in which feminist networkers and the many different Internet actants act in concert.

Today's feminist networkers face the challenge of considering the differences between women and the sceptical attitudes towards group identities. Furthermore, they have to cope with reductions of funding and, as a conesquence, with pressure of time and costs. Accordingly, their political power and influence has decreased. The Internet is designed and constructed, among other places, within these networks; at the same time it intervenes in an idiosyncratic manner as an actant, supporting and disrupting everyday feminist activities. On the one hand, it eases finding and publishing a lot of information and empowers feminist politics; on the other hand, it presents new tasks, is time-consuming and demanding.

Our research project showed that one of the most important concerns of the feminists we interviewed was the wish for better structure of information in the WWW, as the flood of information is perceived as annoying. We therefore developed the idea of a virtual neighbourhood to support empowerment and to adapt the Internet to the needs of the feminist activists. Virtual neighbourhoods can give activists an immediate overview of the varied informative and interactive projects on offer. This is particularly important for feminist networks, considering their low level of material and time resources. At the same time, new problems arise; the structuring of information in particular requires categorisation, which is problematical in the light of the feminist debates concerning group identities.

The Internet is by no means an empowering force per se. It is not a complete and given technology, but can be altered and designed in many ways. It represents an incomplete and interim result of social negotiation processes that is open to other interpretations. The Internet and feminist networks permanently materialise themselves and create new constellations, in all their contradictions, depending on each another. They can thus, as stakeholders in political processes, prompt shifts in existing power structures and strengthen feminist politics.

References

Archibald, Jacqueline; Emms, Judy; Grundy, Frances; Payne, Janet; Turner, Eva (eds.) (2005): The Gender Politics of ICT. Middlesex: Middlesex University Press.

Bijker, Wiebe E.; Hughes, Thomas P.; Pinch, Trevor (eds.) (1987): The social construction of technological systems. Cambridge, MA: MIT Press.

Butler, Judith (1990): Gender trouble. Feminism and the subversion of identity. New York: Routledge.

Butler, Judith (1993): Bodies that matter. On the discursive limits of "sex". New York: Routledge.

Carstensen, Tanja (2005): Die interpretative Herstellung des Internet. Eine empirische Analyse technikbezogener Deutungsmuster am Beispiel gewerkschaftspolitischer Diskurse. Dissertation Department Sozialwissenschaften der Universität Hamburg.

Carstensen, Tanja; Winker, Gabriele (2005a): A tool but not a medium. Practical use of the internet in the women's movement. In: Archibald et al. (2005): 149-162.

Carstensen, Tanja; Winker, Gabriele (2005b): Problemorientierte Suchstrategien und die Auffindbarkeit frauenpolitischer Inhalte im Internet. In: Schachtner, Winker (2005): 91-106.

Drüeke, Ricarda; Winker, Gabriele (2005): Neue Öffentlichkeiten durch frauenpolitische Internet-Auftritte. In: Schachtner, Winker (2005): 31-49.

Frey Steffen, Therese; Rosenthal, Caroline; Väth, Anke (eds.) (2004): Gender Studies. Wissenschaftstheorien und Gesellschaftskritik. Würzburg: Königshausen & Neumann.

Funder, Maria; Dörhöfer, Steffen; Rauch, Christian (eds.) (2005): Jenseits der Geschlechterdifferenz? Geschlechterverhältnisse in der Informations- und Wissensgesellschaft. München/Mering: Hampp.

Graumann, Sigrid; Schneider, Ingrid (eds.) (2003): Verkörperte Technik – Entkörperte Frau. Biopolitik und Geschlecht. Frankfurt: Campus.

Haraway, Donna (1991): Simians, cyborgs, and women. The reinvention of nature. New York: Routledge.

Latour, Bruno (1996): On Actor-Network Theory. A few clarifications. In: Soziale Welt 47: 369-382.

MacKenzie, Donald; Wajcman, Judy (eds.) (1999): The social shaping of technology. 2nd edition. Maidenhead/Philadelphia: Open University Press.

Paulitz, Tanja (2005): Netzsubjektivitäten. Konstruktionen von Vernetzung als Technologien des sozialen Selbst. Eine empirische Untersuchung in Modellprojekten der Informatik. Münster: Westfälisches Dampfboot.

Rappaport, Julian (1984): Studies in Empowerment. Steps towards Understanding and Action. New York: Haworth Press.

Schachtner, Christina; Winker, Gabriele (eds.) (2005): Virtuelle Räume – neue Öffentlichkeiten. Frauennetze im Internet. Frankfurt: Campus.

Singer, Mona (2003): Wir sind immer mittendrin: Technik und Gesellschaft als Koproduktion. In: Graumann, Schneider (2005): 110-124.

Straube, Gregor (2004): Handlungsfähigkeit, Materialität und Politik. Die politischen Theorien von Judith Butler und Donna Haraway. In: Frey et al. (2005): 123-138.

Taube, Wolfgang; Winker, Gabriele (2005): Virtuelle Nachbarschaften zur Unterstützung subalterner Gegenöffentlichkeiten. In: Schachtner, Winker (2005): 107-123.

Wajcman, Judy (2004) TechnoFeminism. Cambridge: Polity Press.

Winker, Gabriele (2005a): Ko-Materialisierung von vergeschlechtlichten Körpern und technisierten Artefakten: Der Fall Internet. In: Funder et al. (2005): 157-178.

Winker, Gabriele (2005b): E-Empowerment – Vielfalt und Integration frauenpolitischer Aktivitäten im Internet. In: Schachtner, Winker (2005): 21-30.

Acknowledgements

We would like to thank Katy Derbyshire for her translation.

Implicit/Explicit Alliances between Gender and Technology in the Construction of Virtual Networks

Tanja Paulitz

Today, very different forms of computer networks, mainly the Internet, are used for professional, political and/or inter-organizational "virtual cooperation". The Internet appears here as a phenomenon in which current social transformation processes crystallize, making them accessible for social science research as if under a magnifying glass. It is the place where social knowledge of what a network is, how it functions and what it means for people to be linked in a network is actually under construction. I assume that the design of Internet technologies necessarily includes social constructions of the understanding of the users and of their subjectivity. This relationship between the design of technology and the social construction of subjectivity is of particular importance in the field of networking technologies since they are, more than other technologies, based on the activity of their users. In short: Networking without active participants is doomed to fail. That means that the elaboration of networking goes along with new conceptions of how people should understand themselves especially as social beings, i.e. in relation to others. Furthermore, today's technology development processes need to be seen in connection with extensive social transformations that are often described in the social sciences with key words like "network-", "information-" and "knowledge-" society (see e.g. Castells 1996). Current tendencies in social theory also diagnose new conceptualizations of the subject. Accordingly, they are sociological analyses of the current discursive order of knowledge, which constitutes the formations of subjectivity and also the epistemic framework for the development of Internet technologies. Inversely, I understand the development of network technologies as a vital part of the formation of this order of knowledge. In this sense, this article is also a result of my engagement in the discussion on the co-construction of technology and society, focusing especially on the constructions of subjectivity.

I carried out a larger-scale empirical study of the construction of networks and subjectivity in the context of the development of "virtual" cooperative spaces (Paulitz 2005). In this article I will take a closer look at the results of the study from a gender studies perspective. In the following I will concentrate on the conceptions of the procedures (process), i.e. the developers' knowledge of how to run the design process and their understanding of what is adequate and promising. I call this knowledge *process knowledge*. After introducing my theoretical perspective in the first section, I will sketch out my empirical research design in the second part. The third section offers an overview of the three dimensions of the construction process, and finally, I will conclude by presenting methodological considerations for feminist technology studies.

1   Gender in the Design of ICT – Theoretical Considerations

In the past, gender studies that addressed the Internet and technical networks tended to focus on the *use* of technology and the construction of gender in its *application* or on the 'playgrounds' of the Internet.[54] An engagement with questions of development has remained an exception (i.e. Kreutzner/Schelhowe 2003). The study of the *production aspect* of information technology and the associated constructive processes and their gender aspects has primarily been carried out in relation to *computers*[55]. The available literature on the question of women's participation in the technical productivity of society (addressing different areas of engineering) note either the chance of changing traditional technological cultures (see Zachmann 2004) or, inversely, suspect that the new concepts of the process of technology development bring aspects to the fore that are linked to the traditional female gender role and thus could open up new professional opportunities for women (for a critical theoretical perspective, see e.g. Faulkner 2000).

The above mentioned aim was supported by Sadie Plant in her book "Zeros and Ones" (1997) with a particular version for the field of inquiry of the Internet. Not only does the development of information technology in general appear as part of a female tradition, but Plant also deploys the supply of images that the metaphor of the net offers to describe network technology in particular as a women's strategy. However, her attempt to promote knowledge about gender specific difference regarding network technology includes at least one problematic aspect that can be illustrated both against the background of available empirical studies on the development processes of Internet technology as well as in

---

54   See the internationally influential study from Sherry Turkle (1995) that prompted much dis-
      cussion. I would refer to the following recent publications for the coverage of the discussion:
      Kahlert/Kajatin 2004, Schachtner/Winker 2005, Green/Adam 2001.

55   See Turkle 1984; Schachtner 1993. The gender aspect in these studies was important in terms
      of the question of gender-specific aspects of programming styles and strategies of software
      development.

relation to theoretical discussions.[56] Els Rommes (2002) showed in the case of "Amsterdam's digital city", for example, that the simple fact of *women participating as developers* does not necessarily lead to gender aspects being taken into consideration in the design. She thus makes the case for involving women who explicitly contribute a *feminist* perspective in the early phase of design projects. These findings speak clearly, as they point out that a simplified gender-specific interpretation of design processes is in danger of reproducing social gender stereotypes in an essentialist manner and thereby reinforcing them. In terms of feminist and social theory, Judy Wajcman argues in her new book "Technofeminism" (2004) against such tendencies in "cyberfeminism" that try to fix traditional stereotypes of women in the course of the celebration of new technologies. She rightly criticizes them because they essentialize binary gender conceptions. Accordingly, in my research I do not ask about 'female' ways of designing, implementing and/or using technology and do not relate to the net as a 'female' technology. As a consequence, I link my study to such theoretical works in gender studies that grasp *gender as a social construct* (see e.g. Helduser et al.: 2004). My approach to the study of technology development is thus not to ascribe the ways of development to the developers being women or men, but rather to analyze the concepts expressed and used by the developers in the field to determine where and in what way these are gendered. This means, on the one hand, reconstructing the characteristics of the specific order of knowledge relating to network technology design and, on the other hand, taking a closer look at their gender aspects. From a theoretical point of view, interlinking these reconstructions also offers methodological insights for feminist technology studies.

2   Qualitative analysis of developers´ process knowledge

I consider these questions in my empirical investigation on "virtual cooperation". Technical platforms that facilitate virtual cooperation have arisen in recent years as a crowded field of research and practice. I will address the question posed on the basis of my qualitative research in two model projects in the area of the *design-oriented* computer science. The model projects were the *Virtuelle Internationale Frauen Universität* (Vifu, transl: Virtual International Women's University) on the one hand and the *Virtueller Druck und Medien-Verbund* (VDM, transl. Virtual Print and Media Association) on the other hand. The Vifu

---

56   See the following for a critique of Plant´s extremely broadly cited position from the perspective of German gender studies: www.heise.de/tp/deutsch/pop/topic_3/4120/1.html and www. txt.de/blau/blau19/plant.htm.

project aimed at developing an Internet server for the international cooperation of scientists and activists in gender studies and women's politics. It was connected to the *Internationale Frauen Universität* (ifu, transl. international women's university) in Hanover in the summer of 2000 and provided technological infrastructure for the participants. The VDM project was conducted in the years 2000 and 2001. It supported cooperation among small businesses and freelancers in the print and media branch. The small firms were cooperating in a local context, in a regional setting. For my study, I linked these two projects under the label "virtual cooperation". They both developed software on the basis of Internet technologies for decentralized cooperative work in different fields. The comparison of the two case studies also made it possible to contrast them in relation to the relevance of gender (among other things).

Table 1: Short chronology of services developed

Vifu	VDM
1. web server (presentation and information of the organization)	1. message board as an interactive web-application
2. discussion forum and mailing lists	2. incremental extension to a virtual work-space:
3. personal homepages, link directories, presentations of research projects	- user administration tool,
4. expert data base	- decentralized data storage,
5. e-mail service	- electronic job ticket
6. local search engine	- discussion forum
7. virtual foto gallery	

I examined both projects over the course of about one year each for my study. The heart of my empirical material is composed of qualitative, semi-structured interviews (based on a set of guiding questions), which I carried out with members of the staff in both model projects at different stages of the developmental process. I asked about patterns and images underlying the technical construction as well as about the experience with these patterns during the implementation of the products. This empirical material was analyzed on the basis of grounded theory (see Strauss 1994/1998), a research style that is suitable for the reconstructtion of everyday theories and interpretations in the field. This means that I moved the statements of the developers themselves into the center of my consideration: I analyzed their arguments for particular constructive procedures and design decisions, their ways of problematizing what they regard as "correct" or, alternatively, as inappropriate procedures for establishing virtual cooperation and how they perceive the users acquiring (or not) the offered technology. Theoretically speaking: The ways of working through the networking "construction site" and the orders of knowledge that emerged in the developers' praxis became the material for my analysis. I understand them in a social scientific sense as local forms of expression of knowledge as well as a situated generation of knowledge.

3   Constructive practices – three dimensions

In my research I discovered three ways in which the interviewees conceptualize the design process: it concerns the production, firstly, on the level of the design of technical applications (3.1); secondly, on the level of training and acquisition of technical knowledge (3.2); and, thirdly, on the level of the content, group-oriented and technology organizing production (3.3). In the following I will focus on the constructions of gender in the conceptualizations of the design process (a question I posed at the beginning of this article). Therefore I cannot describe each model project's perspective in detail, but have to concentrate on more or less compressed case comparisons.

3.1 The technical construction dimension

The software designers in both case studies made an attempt at participatory software development with a specific connection to the product: network technology. From the vifu developer's perspective, the ideal of running the process appears as an experimental cooperative mode of creating and designing applications. Such a model is, for example, underlying the way in which the design process of the so-called expert database on the Vifu server is described. Here, the interviewees characterize it specifically as a process with non-hierarchical positions for developers and participating users. In the beginning, the developers tried to constitute the work in creating a *common* direction together *with* the users through an exchange about user needs and technical possibilities. The ideas and agenda of all participants were reflected and integrated into the process. This experimental way of development is, with some context-specific variation, exemplary for the VDM project as well. Two aspects were emphasized:

- All participants need to develop their perspectives and ideas and reinterpret their own ideas thereby in this process. This makes possible a common space for ideas, in which the technical and social aspects were integrated. It is open for modifications.
- Construction appears explicitly as an (socially and materially) integrated action that cannot be intentionally and indiscriminately controlled by indi-

vidual actors. It is dependent on engagement and initiative, linked to many partial agreements and to the available technical basis.

The analysis thus illustrated that this concept is marked by the agenda of the productivity of social exchange. Vifu explicitly established a specific reference to the social category "gender" from the position of political empowerment: The goal is to integrate women into an *experimental, open technical design process.* Such a reference to gender is absent in the VDM project.

Conversely, as the case comparison shows, both model projects have in common that this experimental way of developing is understood especially as an appropriate manner to produce *network* technology. This means, on the one hand, that the gendering of the technical construction process in Vifu is a political link to women's empowerment in the field of technology. In addition to the possibility of addressing the gender aspect, the concrete process concepts are, on the other hand, also linked to the specifics of the technical product (i.e. creating networks). I will elaborate on this point in the next section.

3.2 The training dimension

The developers undertook various measures in order to increase the participation of the target group members in the virtual activities.

The Vifu developers stressed in the interviews that they planned and carried out an extensive package of measures aimed at the training of the participants. They argued especially that their target group was made up of an international group of women whose technical competencies were unknown to the developers in the planning phase of the project. The suspected specificity of the Vifu user group and the explicitly feminist perspective of the developers were crucial for having training activities *planned* into the project. Whereas the target group in the Vifu project was the object of intense reflection and planning, the technical competencies of the primarily male pilot users in the target group at the start of the VDM project was not made an issue in any important way. The assumption that they would be dealing with technically savvy pilot users could not be confirmed in the course of the project. The developers offered supplementary training measures. However, these activities – introduced more or less as an afterthought – were motivated primarily by the branch-specific stand of technical knowledge.

The difference in addressing the target groups becomes obvious in the comparison of the two case studies.

Additionally, the analysis shows that the *method* of training and the goals associated with training favored in both projects were quite similar in terms of the *conception regarding content*. For example, the developers in both projects noted the necessity of imparting knowledge about network technology and new media in a playful way. An active, experimental learning seemed to them to be more conducive to understanding the principles of the technology and to acquiring self-confidence in applying the technology. Common to both is the departure from the concept of a purely instrumental stance towards technology. The question of content thus illustrates that the concrete strategies for training cannot be understood only as a concern for feminist positions. Rather, the procedure in the case comparison shows that it is a requirement that has a great deal to do with the ideas about how network technology functions, i.e. that it is *network* specific.

One difference does, however, become clear in regard to the social framework of developing competencies. The VDM project worked primarily with the concept of on-the-job training or with forms of individual acquisition of skills. In contrast, the Vifu understood establishing technical competencies increasingly as a continuous process of decentralized, mutual support of the networking actors; a process that, in principle, never ends. The developers called this the move to a *networking* form of training, in which women educate one another themselves. They portray the guiding principle of multipliers in a feminist perspective. These are seen, among other things, as "model citizens" in the new electronic public spheres who are working in different places all over the world. For the Vifu, the technologies of the Internet are acquired by the participants through their social networks.

The analysis of these two dimensions of constructive practices discussed so far shows that gender is brought into the discussion and becomes an object of the development process from a feminist perspective at the moment in which networking is understood as a *technical* activity. In contrast, the male target group appears as generally unmarked when technical activity is concerned. The interview partners were apparently unable to formulate a need for further technical qualification based on gender, but rather based on other, context-related grounds. In the case of VDM, the implicit "equation between masculinity and technology" seems to be again extremely durable, although there are "mismatches between image and practice" (see Faulkner 2000). It is striking that not networking in general, but rather especially the concrete development and implementation of *technology* was *gender coded* for a female target group.

Political empowerment approaches in computer science are thus always forced to manage a difficult balancing act: This was the case with Vifu, where the developers analyzed the asymmetrical social alliance between gender and technology. They worked out ways to change the current conditions. At the same time, they critically reflected on the possible additional effect that they might be reproducing stereotypical assumptions like that a project with a female target group cannot feel confident about having technically savvy users. Such a gendering disappears into the background when we take a closer look at the production processes on the level of the *conception regarding content*. As described above, a quite similar order of knowledge moves to the fore.

3.3   The content dimension

A third level of construction can also be found in the interviews. My material suggests that the processes, generally identified as network *usage* in academic discussions, can instead be interpreted as a *constructive action*. The developers in both projects report on their attempts to encourage active participation. They articulate the necessity that the so-called "user" actually has to create the network. The production of networks only takes place when the participants verbally express themselves, when they relate to one another, when they link their information, and finally, when they also organize the technical surrounding themselves, managing and continuously developing it. I thus interpret such productive actions as co-constructive practices of networking. These practices are not only related to the further development of the technical platform, but also to the production of the social structure of relationships. Regulation and intervention on the part of the developers are not done with the intention to confine, but rather to support and encourage particular actions by the network participants. The interview partners stated that networking emerges as a continuous, iterative process. The result of such a perpetual production is the network itself. The main characteristics of such a productive praxis are as follows:

- The result of the co-construction emerges through continuous participation. Active, communicative subjectivities are required here, i.e. the development of participants who actively network is necessary.
- Particular attention is paid to the functioning of technology on the one hand and the functioning of cooperation, i.e. the social aspects, on the other hand. Both are the object of analysis and development. Technology and sociality are intrinsically linked objects of continuous co-construction.
- The result of the production process is understood as being *procedural*. It is interpreted as a *process* of the perpetual creation of networks itself, as a technology of a networking subjectivity.

As a consequence, my study offers preliminary evidence for a new understand-ding of processes in software development, connected to the new form of ICT described with the term "network". The constructive practices tend to shift from product-orientation to process-orientation. The procedures of construction can be described as practices that go far beyond the development of technology (in the limited sense of the word). As a result, the production of an electronic network actively produces networking subjectivity. The procedures of construction aim at least at *technologies of networking* in a broader sense of the notion "technology".

The case studies differ in the exact emphasis on the construction of networking subjectivity: On the one hand, Vifu wants to contribute to the women being independent producers of networks who become visible through presentations on the web. VDM, on the other hand, aimed at creating a concept of the active, cooperative entrepreneur who cares for more than the presentation of the individual business. This entrepreneur should engage actively in the project in a responsible, caring manner. Such results suggest that the subtext of the statements here also articulate aspects of social exchange that are gender coded and that the developers propose as a normative perspective of change. To overstate it somewhat, this is about female participants in Vifu clearly promoting their own interests and their own profiles by relating to others. The male pioneer users are called upon, in contrast, to concentrate more on the needs of others. This gender dimension becomes even more explicit in the perspective of empowerment in the Vifu. Such a feminist position intends to destabilize traditional gender conceptions. They want *new* representations of women to be visible on the web, and they want to support *new* constructions of subjectivity, i.e. new self-conceptions of female network participants that do not reproduce stereotypical patterns. In contrast, the non-traditional conception of subjectivity in the VDM project is not founded in a feminist orientation. Gender is not even explicitly mentioned here. It becomes visible as an implicit dimension in the developers' constructive orientation when they express their normative ideas about how to create virtual cooperation on the level of co-construction. The developers worked out what was lacking and broached the issue of new necessary aspects of subjectivity during the interview, mainly by relating their observations of how the pioneer users interact in the virtual workspace. They perceive freelancers and small business employees as usually acting for the interests of their own organization. In order to support the creation of a virtual team, the VDM developers emphasized such specific kinds co-constructive practices that are traditionally more or less femininely coded social competencies.

4   Conclusion – Methodological Considerations

To conclude, I will point out some theoretical and methodological aspects of my gender analysis of process knowledge presented here:

Firstly, this study reaffirms an issue that feminist technology studies have repeatedly brought up: Gender is present even when it is not explicitly expressed, as in the VDM case. In my comparative case study I intend to make such gender dimensions visible. Methodologically speaking, I tried to analyze implicit constructions of gender on the basis of empirical research without assuming and fixing a binary gender order in advance. This aims at reconstructing the unexpressed gendered assumptions in process knowledge.

Secondly, the comparison of Vifu with a non-feminist oriented model project makes obvious that Vifu's strategies for empowerment of women in technology should not be confused with notions of 'female' manners of technology design and networking. The Vifu case shows that the emphasis on breaking down traditional boundaries is a balancing act that entails addressing gender issues and stereotypes in technology in the course of a concrete design project without essentializing the practiced design procedures.

Thirdly, several similarities in the process knowledge on the level of technical construction, training and co-construction show that there are patterns of a new order of knowledge relating to the specific field of networking technology and the context of broader discursive constellations in current societies. Feminist projects do not stand outside of these contexts. In fact they are always part of those constellations (whose implicit genderings have to be identified like we have seen in the case of VDM). They act inside of the frameworks of the prevailing order of knowledge, but also have (limited) means to use transformations in a *strategic* way to deconstruct traditional boundaries in the field of technology.

References

Castells, Manuel (1996): The Information Age: Economy, Society, and Culture. 1: The Rise of the Network Society. Cambridge/Mass.
Faulkner, Wendy (2000): The Power and the Pleasure? A Research Agenda for Making Gender Stick to Engineers. In: Science, Technology & Human Values 25 (1): 87-119.
Funken, Christiane (1998): Neue Berufspotentiale für Frauen in der Software-Entwicklung. In: Oechtering, Veronika; Winker, Gabriele (eds.): Computernetze - Frauenplätze. Frauen in der Informationsgesellschaft. Opladen: 57-66.
Green, Eileen; Adam, Alison (eds.) (2001): Virtual Gender. Technology, Consumption and Identity Matters. New York.

Helduser, Urte; Marx, Daniela; Paulitz, Tanja; Pühl, Katharina (eds.) (2004): Under construction? Konstruktivistische Perspektiven in feministischer Theorie und For-
schungspraxis. Frankfurt/M., New York.
Kahlert, Heike; Kajatin, Claudia (eds.) (2004): Arbeit und Vernetzung im Informations-
zeitalter. Wie neue Technologien die Geschlechterverhältnisse verändern. Frank-
furt/M., New York.
Kreutzner, Gabriele; Schelhowe, Heidi (eds.) (2003): Agents of Change. Virtuality, Gender, and the Challenge to the Traditional University. Opladen.
Paulitz, Tanja (2005): Netzsubjektivitäten. Konstruktionen von Vernetzung als Technologien des sozialen Selbst. Eine empirische Untersuchung in Modellprojekten der In-
formatik. Münster, London.
Rommes, Els (2002): Creating Places for Women on the Internet. The Design of a
Women's Square in a Digital City. In: The European Journal of Women's Studies 9
(4): 400-429.
Schachtner, Christel (1993): Geistmaschine. Faszination und Provokation am Computer.
Frankfurt/Main.
Schachtner, Christina; Winker, Gabriele (eds.) (2005): Virtuelle Räume – neue Öffent-
lichkeiten. Frauennetze im Internet. Frankfurt/M., New York.
Strauss, Anselm L. (1998 [1994]): Grundlagen qualitativer Sozialforschung. Datenanalyse
und Theoriebildung in der empirischen und soziologischen Forschung. München.
Turkle, Sherry (1984): The Second Self. Computers and the Human Spirit. New York.
Turkle, Sherry (1995): Life on the Screen: Identity in the Age of the Internet. New York.
Wajcman, Judy (2004): Technofeminism. Cambridge.
Zachmann, Karin (2004): Mobilisierung der Frauen. Technik, Geschlecht und Kalter
Krieg in der DDR. Frankfurt/M., New York.

IV Education and Empowerment for the Information Society

Bridging Disciplines: Gender Studies and Computer Science in an E-Learning Course

Ruth Meßmer, Sigrid Schmitz

1 Theoretical Background: Gender, Technology and E-Learning

1.1 Gender & technology or "Things are in a constant state of flux"

E-learning is an important way of learning in the universities and workplaces of today and tomorrow. It is an interesting field for feminist researchers as well: On the one hand we analyze, how the technology generates new or other gender effects than in traditional learning situations. On the other hand we discuss whether it can open new didactical and technological possibilities to de-construct gender-stereotypes and foster more diversity.

Dealing with gender aspects in e-learning initially requires a closer look at how gender is created in society, at the construction of technology and the interdependencies of both. Feminist theories and research have shown that gender is a constitutional category of society confirming and reproducing the existing social structures. Crucial for feminist analyses of the last decades were e.g. the works of Judith Butler (1990), and Candace West and Don Zimmermann (1987). From different theoretical backgrounds, both claimed that gender is not an essential attribute of individuals but something that is 'done' or 'performed'. It is being produced through interaction and it structures interaction. Consequently, gender phenomena and gender identities are not fixed but have to be negotiated in every social situation anew; they are contingent. Constructivist research focuses therefore on the question of how gender is being produced in interactions. These feminist approaches focus on gender segregation in the labour market, in private and public space, in behaviour and in gender roles. They criticize dichotomous gender manifestation and the current naturalization of gender stereotypes that uses biological and essentialist arguments for male and female skills, attitudes, motivations, etc.[57]

---

[57] These argumentations are underlined recently with reference to modern brain research (for overview see Schmitz 2004).

Taking into account that firstly, neither women nor men can be treated as a homogenous category while a network of overlapping factors (e. g. age, class, ethnicity, social and economic status) influences gender in performance and that secondly, gender identities are fragmented and in flux, we consequently move from gender to diversity. With regard to e-learning, Regina Claus et al. (2004) define diversity as "all the differences between the parties involved that affect the process of learning and teaching". 'Doing gender' here means, these differences are not seen as fixed aspects but as expressions of a specific situation and interaction.

Feminist technology studies (e.g. Green et al. 1993, Schinzel 1999; Rommes et al. 2004) and other researchers have found that technology is a social construction as well. Social phenomena are incorporated into technology itself; not only in their artefacts, but also in their techniques, models, knowledge, and so on. Gender and technology abide in close relationship. The notion of "co-construction of gender and technology" does not only imply that they are both fluid and negotiable, but also that they are constructed with reference and in relation to each other (Wajcman 2004: 107). Experiences with gendered technologies are always embedded in gendered societal, cultural, and power relations. They induce gendered strategies in interaction with information technology.

In consequence, a feminist view on e-learning should investigate gendered structures in didactics and technology without reproducing stereotypes. It should search for inclusion strategies by:

- focusing on the diversity of users (not only gender but also age, class, ethnicity, social and economic status, for example, and their interrelation) and creating conditions which support their various demands on technology and
- concentrating on the process of gender construction in the interactive field between users and e-learning technology, using a fluid concept of identity by considering the context of the practices in which they occur.

Flexibility and fluidity of gender and technology incorporate not only the facets of 'performing' and 'doing gender' along stereotyped categories. They also have the potential to break through the gender stereotypes, to cross the gender borders, to ignore, withstand or confuse gender dichotomies. Butler labelled this deconstructive force 'performativity' in contrast to the 'performance' of gender stereotypes (Butler 1993, 2004). Another approach was, for example, Donna Haraway's cyborg vision (Haraway 1985), that technology and humanity form a symbiotic relationship. Although Haraway's vision of breaking down nature-culture binaries as well as gendered dichotomies within the technology-humanity symbiosis seems to fall short of the reality of the modern information technology world, her cyborg metaphor depicted the relatedness of the categories quite clearly. The cyborg vision can be seen as a precursor to the idea of co-construction of gender and technology.

For this reason it is not only important to make the gender constructions and performances transparent by critical analyses, but even more important to develop new forms of performativities that allow for diversity instead of gender binaries. A closer look at gender and technology often proves that diverse rather than stereotyped behaviour is performed in interaction with information technologies. Making the diversity visible is therefore one way to de-construct gender stereotypes.

Concerning e-learning, this points to an integration of the results of gender research into teaching and an attempt at new forms of learning, to test some of the developed gender-sensitive approaches in e-learning technology (Schmitz & Meßmer 2005; Meßmer & Schmitz 2004) in real teaching/learning scenarios. We started one approach that outlines diversity aspects and the co-construction of gender and technology within interdisciplinary e-learning courses, where the students could play with gender roles and technical facilities. With this approach we tried to fill the 'critical transformative room' between e-learning technology and the users (Crutzen 2003) with discerning human beings. In the following chapter, we summarize some results of gender and e-learning research and the consequential gender-sensitive and diversity-oriented user demands (for an overview see Schmitz et al. 2006) which we tried to integrate into our courses.

1.2   Gender and E-Learning

Questions which had mostly been answered in traditional teaching arose and had to be answered again in relation to virtual learning processes.

One question refers to the access to and permanence in e-learning, e.g. how does technology change access to learning and who is excluded, who is included? The level of computer literacy is mentioned quite often as an obstacle for women. Gender effects emerge, but they are highly influenced by age, education, income, and the field of work (e.g. (N)Onliner 2003, Norris 2001). Roughly speaking, well educated and young women have almost as much computer literacy as the corresponding group of men. The 'digital gap' widens the older, poorer and less educated women are. A gender-sensitive course should therefore consider the skills of the target group. Due to the diversity approach, it is advisable to use technology that includes all learners with different levels of computer literacy instead of using highly complex software and huge systems that assume a certain technological knowledge. Most suitable are systems which can be extended successively according to the changing expertise of the users

(Meßmer et al 2003). A good introduction to e-learning tools and permanent and encouraging tutoring is also essential for a successful e-learning course (Wiesner et al. 2004).

Other questions concern how new media change learning cultures and methods (e.g. the absence of the body, the change from oral to written communication) and the consequences for gender aspects. What role can e-learning play for the development of new learning and teaching methods? With respect to the recent change in pedagogy from an instructional to a constructivist paradigm, many feminist demands for a 'women-friendly' pedagogy now seem to transform into demands for 'learner-friendly' didactics in general. Instructional teaching methods work with the idea that the knowledge of a teacher is passed on to students. On the contrary, constructivist teaching and learning concepts hold the belief that learners construct knowledge individually, based on their own unique experiences. Therefore it is important to take into account the diversity of prior experiences, personal interests, and different learning styles. According to constructivist approaches students take an active and explorative role in the learning process; communication and cooperation are of major significance (Reinmann-Rothmeier & Mandl 1999) since working in social interaction promotes students to develop and discuss various viewpoints of the content presented in their course. Cooperative learning is a demand of feminist pedagogues as well. Several research studies state preferences of women to work in groups (e.g. AAUW 2000, Rajagopal & Bojin 2003). Furthermore, a stable virtual community building process seems to prevent women from dropping out (Wiesner 2001; for a detailed discussion of group working aspects in e-learning see: Schmitz & Messmer 2005). E-learning systems which offer technical facilities for cooperative work, e.g. Computer Supported Cooperative Learning-Systems (CSCL), and of course, the integration of group work in the didactics of the course support both constructivist and gender-sensitive learning.

Cooperative work and collaborative learning require an enhanced communication effort. Gender effects in computer mediated communication were examined by various researchers (e.g. Herring 2000). Several studies stated gender-specific effects in the way that men dominated the communication by means of length and frequency of messages and by their communication style. However, the surveys vary concerning the extent of differences and the occurrence of single gender effects, thus implying a high context dependency of communication via computer. Savicki et al. proved the existence of varying gender effects in different gender ratios in groups (Savicki et al. 1996). Other variables such as, for example, anonymity and level of professionalism influence communication as well. Cornelius (2002) found that information about the individual and about the professional status and expertise of a person diminished gender effects. Some surveys also showed differences in the communication facilities that were preferred. In some contexts there seems to be a preference of women to communicate in a non-public or semi-public way. Therefore it is advisable to provide for various communication channels, e.g. email, messenger, chat, forum (see Schmitz & Meßmer 2005).

A third set of questions refers to the importance of interdisciplinarity and expertise: In interdisciplinary teaching and learning settings, students and teachers are urged to discuss and reflect their own disciplinary language, their disciplinary theories and settings, their roles and habitus. In this way, the experience and knowledge of the learners can be included in the course concept. This is not only a demand of constructivist pedagogy, but one of feminist pedagogues, as they claim to create discourses from the experience of the learners and to use concrete and practical examples in teaching (e.g. Schinzel & Ruiz Ben 2002; Wiesner et al. 2004).

We have chosen the three facets interaction with technology, collaborative work and interdisciplinarity for a course concept to evaluate approaches of gender-sensitive and diversity-oriented e-learning in practice.

2   Courses on Gender and E-Learning: Concepts and Results

2.1   Concept

We held two courses at the University of Freiburg, one in the winter term 2004/2005 and one in the summer term 2005. The courses were blended learning courses, meaning that they included virtual working phases as well as face-to-face sessions. The aim of these courses was to open up a field of learning where students of different disciplines had to work collaboratively, not only on IST topics, but also with computer technologies.

Course topics: The topics of the courses combined the issues 'gender' and 'e-learning'. The first course was called "E-Learning between demands and reality: concepts of gender and diversity". The second course was entitled "Who learns how with new media? Demands and concepts for Learning Management Systems". Both course topics set focus on questions of gender-sensitive and diversity-oriented demands on e-learning technology.

Interdisciplinary student groups: One decisive aspect of the concept of our courses was to bring Computer Science students (CS students) and Gender Studies students (GS students) together, both as experts in their respective fields. With the course topics we aimed to meet the interests of CS students in user-oriented e-learning development and the interests of GS students in gender and technology. The inclusion of their different experiences and the interdisciplinary dialogue was part of the attempt to deconstruct gender dichotomies. The CS students participated in the courses to gain credit points for "Computer Science and Social Studies" as part of their CS curriculum. The students of Social and Cultural Science studies had "Gender Studies" as a minor alongside their main discipline. For all participants the courses were facultative, thus CS students could have chosen other courses in the topics of technology without gender aspects and GS students could have chosen gender topics without technology. Thus, the students who finally attended the courses were motivated and interested in the combination of gender and IST.

Interaction with technology: One general principle of both courses was the combination of theoretical analyses of state of the art research in the field of 'gender and e-learning' with empirical analyses of e-learning platforms and groupware systems and with their own experience with e-learning technology. Every course consisted of four sequential parts supported by a groupware tool[58], to which all students got a face-to-face introduction and an online tutorial. The groupware system facilitated access to a content management system, communication services (e-mail, forum, chat) and personalized user information.

- The course started with the joint creation of an e-learning glossary. This way we ensured that every student gained the same level of knowledge on technical and didactical terms concerning e-learning. The participants then developed a concept map of the terms related to 'gender and e-learning'. Based on this concept map, they decided on particular topics for the following research analysis:
- The analyses of particular research topics (e.g. learning theories and their implementation in e-learning, computer mediated communication, cultural aspects, personalization attempts in e-learning, amongst others) had to be carried out in working groups who could collaborate and communicate in the groupware system. The results of the particular research topics were presented in a face-to-face session to the other students of the course. On the basis of these research results, a *list of demands* for gender-sensitive and diversity-oriented e-learning technology was compiled.
- In the third part of the course, new working groups were formed which then compared and evaluated e-learning platforms and group working systems according to the list of demands. Next, the students had to use demo or guest accounts of current e-learning systems. They explored the technical aspects and facilities of the systems; they 'played' with the technology.

---

58   In both courses we worked with our groupware system eGoware, http://egoware.de.

Again, the working groups had to collaborate, communicate and prepare a presentation of their results. Then we provided a collaborative text editor, a wiki-room[59], which was introduced to the students in a face-to-face session.
- During the fourth part of the course, the working groups combined the results of the theoretical research analyses and the empirical systems analyses and had to write a final report together in a wiki-document. They were also called on to revise the presentations of the other groups by asking questions and commenting on their presentation concepts in the forum of the groupware tool (eGoware).

Collaborative work and role distribution: We emphasized collaborative work in the concept of the courses and the students had to change groups. In the first group they focused on a specific topic of e-learning theory and were then, in the second empirical group, 'experts' for their field of research. This approach guaranteed that the knowledge they had already acquired was distributed to the others. As a second effect, the switching of groups mixed GS students with CS students, as the first groups consisted mostly of students from the same discipline.

2.2 Some Observations

The majority of the Computer Science students who participated in our courses were male (6 males in the winter course, 7 males and 1 female in the summer course) and the majority of Gender Studies students were female (9 females in the winter course, 3 females and 2 males in the summer course). The collaborative and discursive work of these students showed some interesting outcomes concerning

- the questions of access to and permanence in e-learning, i.e. the interaction with technology,
- the question of how new media changes learning cultures and methods with a particular focus on collaborative work and gender
- the potential of interdisciplinary learning settings for the reflection on the co-construction of gender and technology (see chapter 1.2).

Interaction with technology: Most of the GS students had neither prior experience with e-learning facilities nor with technical tools that support group

---

59   This virtual working tool enables quick and efficient writing and publishing of texts for a group and supports the development of html documents, for users with minor html programming experience as well.

work. The introduction to a simple and intuitive groupware system helped them to overcome their initial hesitation towards computer technology. Nearly all students found it easy to work with the groupware system eGoware.

After the students had worked out a variety of aspects of user demands for e-learning systems and after they organized their first group work in eGoware, they were motivated to evaluate further and partly more advanced systems. Although the GS students sometimes needed the help of the CS students in working with the demos of these systems, they were able to gain access and to acquire an overview of the technical constructions in general. In the empirical evaluations of the technical systems, they obtained a deeper insight into particular functionalities of e-learning tools. In the final course evaluation some GS students stated explicitly that they had overcome barriers to IT through the interaction with e-learning technology.

The CS students, on the other hand, were confronted with questions that reached far beyond purely technological aspects of e-learning systems. They had to cope with the multifaceted aspects that have to be taken into account when technology is to be implemented in society. As some of them stated at the end of the courses, they arrived at conclusions about the limitations in e-learning technology with respect to the user-oriented and gender-sensitive demands they had developed in advance.

During the third part of the courses, we introduced another technical system to facilitate collaborative text editing, the wiki-system. This was a technical challenge for course members with minor computer literacy. However, when the students evaluated the groupware system eGoware as too limited for collaborative text editing, the introduction of a second tool was embedded in their working demands. At the end of the course the participants evaluated both applied systems as more or less adequate for their course tasks. Several students, however, remarked that it was cumbersome that the group working and the text editing functions were not integrated into one system and that they had to switch from one system to the other.

Collaborative work: The first formation of the working groups occurred mostly within the disciplines of CS and GS students. These groups worked on the theoretical papers and research results in e-learning. We then mixed the groups again for the empirical part of the courses, and we arranged them in a way that the new working groups all consisted of females and males, GS students and CS students and 'experts' of different research topics from the theoretical analyses. The new mix of gender and discipline urged the students to interdisciplinary collaboration and communication. At the end of the course, students of both disciplines reported a helpful atmosphere and a reduction of prejudices against each other that was promoted by interdisciplinary group work.

The tools for collaboration and communication were used in a hetero-geneous way, in other words, not always along the disciplinary or gender border. Nearly all of the students preferred e-mail or forum communication. In the first working groups there were CS students who knew each other well and preferred to meet face-to-face to prepare their presentation. In the third part of the course only one mixed group used the chat for one online meeting but then met face-to-face again in the following. When asked about their apathy towards the chat facilities in the final course evaluation, they stated that they found face-to-face meetings more effective for preparing their presentation. On the other hand, there was a female GS student in the winter course who started with minor computer literacy and had to leave for some time to Nigeria during the course. During her absence, she communicated with her working group via the eGoware system and stated this supported her in continuing participation in the course.

Interdisciplinarity: Through the theoretical parts of the courses the students were sensitized to the discussion that technological development has to be related closely to user-oriented demands, not only for gender-sensitivity but also for other group demands, e.g. for people with visual impairment. The interdisci-plinary mix of students in the course and their diverse needs and views made them experience this aspect immediately. Both groups learned something about the discipline-specific thinking and working methods and had to find a way to communicate and cope with interdisciplinarity.

One CS student mentioned that he was impressed with the variety of aspects to be considered when implementing technology into society. He stated that he had not been exposed to such a broad view in 'traditional' Computer Science Courses, not even in IT courses on usability. In the interdisciplinary discussions the CS students had to recognize that the way they spoke about technology was sometimes not understandable to outsiders. They also had to learn that their opinions as technological 'experts' about what is easy to implement or use was mostly not that easy for non-computer specialists. Personally confronted by several GS students, the CS students had to take gender aspects seriously.

The GS students stated that working with technology turned out to be fun and that it was not as difficult as expected. In particular, they mentioned the positive experience of gaining access to the e-learning systems and to understand how they work. They recognized that technology is formed in a special way for specific aims, that technology can be criticized and that it can be changed. As 'experts' for gender questions the GS students learned to explain gender concepts in an understandable way.

3   Gender in e-learning: some primary conclusions

In the two described courses we endeavoured to embed feminist approaches to the co-construction of gender and technology into e-learning scenarios. We did this by promoting a progressive introduction and extension of technology, by sensitizing the students to learner diversity and user needs in e-learning, and by referring to constructivist didactics with a particular focus on interdisciplinary collaborative work. In particular, we emphasised the combination of theoretical and empirical learning in interaction with e-learning technology and the inclusion of students' disciplinary expertise (Computer Science, Gender Studies).

The successive, communicative and group aided process of technological assessment did not only break down initial barriers, it also took the students far into computer technology. Both groups were sensitized to not accepting technology as given and fixed or as 'the one best way' of doing technology. They evaluated and criticized the different e-learning tools with respect to the specific purpose, the context, the target group, etc.

The high degree of collaboration between technology 'experts' and gender 'experts' opened the possibility to reflect not only on discipline-specific imprints but also the challenges and benefits of *interdisciplinary work*. At the same time, the discussions were based on the students' professional standards and thus permitted an interaction predicated on respect. We considered this approach quite successful. Much more than the theoretical preoccupation with diversity, the practical experience with the 'respected difference' seemed to be important. We had the impression that both CS and GS students regarded e-learning technology in a new way after the courses, that they kept in mind how transformable and context-dependent technology is and how perceptions of an imaginary 'user' or 'learning situation' determine the design of e-learning systems.

In chapter one, we pointed out that feminist approaches view gender phenomena and gender identities not as fixed but contingent and to be performed. Additionally, the term co-construction of gender and technology emphasises that gender identity and technology are interrelated, e.g. the connection of male identity to technology in western industrial cultures still exists. Within the scope of our courses there were some interesting 'flashlights' concerning gender identities that we want to mention in closing, although they can only be discussed as tentative evidences due to their limited number of occurrences. The students in our courses could refer to at least two identity concepts, their gender concept and their disciplinary concept. In the beginning of the course, a discipline specific allocation was obvious: Most of the CS students (also the female CS student) focused on the technical aspects of e-learning technology and most of the GS students felt responsible for the didactic aspects of this field of research. That specialization seemed to confirm traditional gender dichotomies generally (Wiesner et al. 2004).

But there were also examples of crossing the typical gender constructions. The one female CS student who chose a technical topic for her course work performed a strong disciplinary identity in this situation. Other male CS students focused on learning theories and didactics in the theoretical part of the course and not on technical aspects. Some female and male GS students were quite skilled with computers and performed these technical competencies in interaction with the other participants. Sometimes these references to gender and disciplinary concept seemed to conflict. Two male GS students, who gave a very good introduction into gender theory, used very technical terms in interdisciplinary discussions and referred frequently to particular technical aspects and functionalities of the e-learning systems in their presentation of the empirical analyses. It seemed that they tried to impress the CS students with their technical knowledge although they came from Gender Studies. We conclude that their male identity conflicted with their discipline. Technology as a crucial part of male identity production may have turned up in the case of these two students very explicitly.

These observations may deliver some first clues about multifaceted identity construction in the field of gender and IT. Another interesting way of dealing with identities was shown by Corneliussen (2004). She analyzed the gendered expectations of male and female students in relation to computers and characterised six positions that are negotiated in the students' discourse ranging between harmony and disharmony with the gendered expectations. This could be a fruitful concept for further investigations on the construction of gender in the field of e-learning. We are still at the outset of the analysis of feminist theoretical approaches to the co-construction of gender and technology in practice. Things are in a constant state of flux: and we may have - at least to a small degree - a say in which direction.

References

AAUW Educational Foundation Research (2000): Tech-Savvy: Educating girls in the new computer age. Washington, DC: AAUW.

Butler, Judith (2004): Undoing Gender. New York, London: Routledge.

Butler, Judith (1993): Bodies that Matter. On the Discursive Limits of "Sex". New York, London: Routledge.

Butler, Judith (1990): Gender Trouble: Feminism and the Subversion of Identity. New York, London: Routledge.

Claus, Regina; Otto, Anne; Schinzel, Britta (2004): Gender Mainstreaming im diversifizierten Feld einer Hochschule: Bedingungen – Akzeptanz – Strategien. Erfahrungen aus dem Notebook-University-Projekt. IIG-Berichte 1/04. URL: http://mod.iig.unifreiburg.de/cms/fileadmin/publikationen/online-publikationen/GruenerBericht-IIG-GM-in-FMoLL.pdf.

Cornelius, Caroline (2002): Your mail, you're female. Geschlechtsidentität im Kontext von textbasierter computervermittelter Kommunikation. In: Bente, Gary; Krämer, Nicole C.; Petersen, Anita (eds): Virtuelle Realitäten. Göttingen, Seattle: Hogrefe: 181-202.

Corneliussen, Hilde (2004): "I don't understand computer programming because I'm a woman!": Negotiating Gendered Positions in a Norwegian Discourse of Computing. In: Morgan, Konrad; Brebbia, Carlos A.; Sanchez, Javier; Voiskuonsky, A. (eds): Human Perspectives in the Internet Society: Culture, Psychology and Gender. Advances in Information and Communication Technologies 4. Wessex: WIT-Press: 173-182.

Crutzen, Cecile (2003): ICT-Representations as Transformative Critical Rooms. In: Kreutzner, Gabriele; Schelhowe, Heidi (eds): Agents of Change. Virtuality, Gender and the Challenge to the Traditional University. Opladen: Leske & Budrich: 87-106.

Green, Eileen; Pain, Den; Owen, Jenny (eds) (1993): Gendered by Design. Information Technology and Office Systems, London: Taylor & Francis.

Haraway, Donna (1985): Manifesto for Cyborgs: Science and Technology, and Socialist Feminism in the 1980's. Socialist Review 80: 65-108.

Herring, Susan (2000): Gender Differences in CMC: Findings and Implications. The CPSR Newsletter, 18/1. Available: http://www.cpsr.org/issues/womenintech/herring.

Meßmer, Ruth; Schmitz, Sigrid (2004): Gender Demands on E-Learning In: Morgan, Konrad; Brebbia, Carlos A.; Sanchez, Javier. & Voiskuonsky, A. (eds): Human Perspectives in the Internet Society: Culture, Psychology and Gender. Advances in Information and Communication Technologies 4. Wessex: WIT-Press: 245-254.

Meßmer, Ruth; Kaiser, Oliver; Taubmann, Christoph; Schmitz, Sigrid; Heidtke, Birgit; Schinzel, Britta (2003): ModUS - a Modular User-Oriented CSCL System in Line with Gender Research. In: Proceedings of E-Learn 2003, World Conference on E-Learning in Corporate, Government, Healthcare, & Higher Education. Phoenix, Arizona, USA, 2337-2340.

(N)Onliner-Atlas 2003. Frauen geben Technik neue Impulse e.V., Initiative D21 & TNS Emnid, (eds) (2003): Internetnutzung von Frauen und Männern in Deutschland 2003. Gender Mainstreaming Sonderauswertung des (N)Onliner-Atlas.

Norris, Pippa (2001): Digital Divide. Civic Engagement, Information Poverty, and the Internet Worldwide. Cambridge: Cambridge University Press.

Rajagopal, Indhu; Bojin, Nis (2003): A Gendered World: Students and Instructional Technologies. First Monday 8 (1): 1-23. Available: http://firstmonday.org/issues/issue8_1/rajagopal/index.html.

Reinmann-Rothmeier, Gabi; Mandl, Heinz (1999): Teamlüge oder Individualisierungsfalle? Eine Analyse kollaborativen Lernens und dessen Bedeutung für die Förderung von Lernprozessen in virtuellen Gruppen. Forschungsbericht Nr. 115. Universität München: Lehrstuhl für Empirische Pädagogik und Pädagogische Psychologie.

Rommes, Els; van Slooten, Irma; van Oost, Ellen; Oudshoorn, Nelly (eds) (2004): Designing Inclusion: The development of ICT products to include women in the Information Society. Available: http://www.rcss.ed.ac.uk/sigis/public/deliverables/D06/1.

Savicki, Viktor; Lingenfelter, Dawn; Kelley, Merle (1996): Gender Language Style and Group Composition in Internet Discussion Groups. Journal of Computer Mediated Communication 2 (3).

Schinzel, Britta; Ruiz Ben, Esther (2002): Gendersensitive Mediendidaktik und Gestaltung von Lernmedien. In: BMBF (ed.): Gender Mainstreaming in der beruflichen Bildung: Anforderungen an Medienpädagogik und Medienentwicklung. Berlin: BMBF, 15-54.

Schinzel, Britta (1999): Informatik, vergeschlechtlicht durch Kultur und Strukturen, ihrerseits vergeschlechtlichend durch die Gestaltung ihrer Artefakte. In: Janshen, Doris (ed.): Frauen über Wissenschaft. Weinheim: Juventus: 61–81.

Schmitz, Sigrid; Meßmer, Ruth (2005): Working in groups: Gender impacts in e-learning. In: Archibald, Jaqueline; Emms, Judy; Grundy, Frances; Payne, Janet; Turner, Eva (Eds.): The Gender Politics of ICT. Middlesex Univ. Press: Middlesex: 265-280.

Schmitz, Sigrid, Messmer, Ruth & Schinzel, Britta (2006): Gender and diversity in e-learning. In: Trauth, Eileen M. (ed.): Gender and Information Technology Encyclopedia. (in press).

Schmitz, Sigrid (2004): Körperlichkeit in Zeiten der Virtualität. In: Schmitz, Sigrid; Schinzel, Britta (Eds.): Grenzgänge: Genderforschung in Informatik und Naturwissenschaften. Königstein: Ulrike Helmer Verlag: 118-132.

Wajcman, Judy (2004): Technofeminism. Cambridge: Blackwell.

West, Candace; Zimmermann, Don H. (1987): Doing Gender. In: Gender & Society 1 (2):125-151.

Wiesner, Heike (2001): Virtuelles Lernen. Das Geschlecht läuft immer mit. Tagung: Frauen und Technologien. Zum Einsatz neuer Medien in der Lehre, Innsbruck, 7./8 Juni 2001. http://fem.uibk.ac.at/nmtagung/a_aufsatz_wiesner.htm.

Wiesner, Heike et al. (2004): Gender Mainstreaming in "Neue Medien in der Bildung" - Leitfaden. http://dimeb.informatik.uni-bremen.de/documents/projekt.gender.GMLeitfaden.pdf.

Computer Games: Playing Gender, Reflecting on Gender

Edeltraud Hanappi-Egger

Gendered Technologies: The Case of Computer Games

The computer game market is one of the strongest in terms of business volume. Nevertheless, a survey conducted by the Computer Entertainment Software Association (CESA) in Japan in 2001 highlights an interesting phenomenon, namely that the number of active game players decreased from 39.3% to 27.8%. The group of "dormant" players consists of 28.1% stating that they are waiting for games they are interested in.

		2001 General Public	1999 General Public
Active Game Players		27.8%	39.3%
Dormant	'I used to play but now stop playing. I want to try again only if any software interests me'	28.1%	23.4%
Prospective	'I have never tried but I want to try if any software interests me'	8.3%	12.2%
Disinterested	'I have never tried and I won't' and 'I used to play but I won't anymore'	35.8%	24.2%

Table 1: Distribution of game players` types in Japan
(source: CESA 2002: 58-62)

The dormant group consists almost evenly of males and females, but the prospective and disinterested customers were mainly females. This means – from a
market point of view in terms of number of consumers– that there is still a large
market potential not satisfied yet. Consequently the question remains how
computer games have to be changed to attract women too.

Hanappi-Egger (2003) shows that gender generally plays an important role
in the discussion on new information and communication technologies. The use
of new technologies is gender-specific, and also in the design of technological
artifacts there is a crucial gender-dimension. Generally for the design and
development of technologies the analogy to the built environment can be drawn.
Wajcman (2001) establishes the connection between the built environment and
patriarchy and shows that cultural assumptions such as gender-specific division
of labor shape the design of spaces. This leads to the fact that e.g. housewives
normally are not provided with own spaces in houses but are assigned to specific
shared rooms such as living room or kitchen. A similar analysis could be made
for computer-systems. Educational programs such as computer sciences are
embedded in specific social contexts including an understanding of the profess-
sion of the computer scientist and of CS as a discipline. Students in computer
science spend much time in studying how to model social contexts, what procedures of software development there are and learning programming languages.
This knowledge strongly determines ways of approaching, observing, selecting
and describing social settings such as work processes. Moreover, engineers are
socially embedded, meaning that they are part of an environment with gender
dimensions such as gender-specific division of labor, role-expectations, and
gender-specific responsibilities. Thus, the conclusion can be drawn that an
engineering perspective – in terms of approaching social reality for the purpose
of modeling – also, even if unconsciously has gender-implications (Hanappi-
Egger 2004a).

Computer games have already been a topic in western feminist discussions,
since for many children playing games is their first contact with computers,
particularly in industrialized countries. These games have the potential to keep
people interested in technological issues, an interest considered important
nowadays. However, computer games are strongly gender-biased; mainly men
play computer games, manly men develop them (see Gorriz, Medina 2000) and
gender-stereotyping is a main feature in computer games. Both facts strengthen
gender barriers. Most researchers agree that – although boys and girls are equally
skilled - boys play more with computers and both sexes consider computers and
computer games as "boys' toys" (see e.g. Cassell, Jenkins 1998). Concerning the
computer game market Weber (2004) shows - based on empirical studies - that
the involved companies are rather gender-blind. Most currently available games

are geared to boys' playing preferences. Even though marketing specialists are aware that girls are less active in copying computer games illegally, they assume that this economic advantage is substituted by the disadvantage that female gamers are not willing to spend as much time and money as boys for computer games. Furthermore, referring to the highly competitive market, game developing companies concentrate on core-competences, respectively on a genre. Since the genre is often action and adventure games, they create gendered exclusion mechanisms and consequently attract specific male gamers. This is so, because at least from a statistical point of view less females are interested in this genre.

Furthermore, new media are used for the formation of ideologies of gender. E.g. Douglas et al. (2002) showed that most video game characters are male and, if they are female, they often are negatively portrayed as helpless and passive actors. Computer games ascribe to female figures limited roles and less space of actions (see also Weber 2004).

Next to the existing critique of sexism in computer games, feminist researchers see interesting opportunities in new media. Features such as multimedia ability, interactivity and 3-dimensional design allow for interesting and innovative experiences. Furthermore, Richard (2003) points out that in the presentation of women in computer games social value systems are expressed, e.g. weakness is not only a question of socialization, but it is also cultivated through ways of dressing, female clothes are less suitable for physical exercise. The analysis of several female heroes such as Betty Boo, Wonder Woman, Barbarella, Emma Peel, Xena, Lara Croft shows that there are multiply-coded dressing languages, combining male with female attributes. Thus they lead to ambiguity and open up a space for reflection. This space provides a focus for feminist discussion. By breaking gendered stereotypes irritation is caused, and irritation can lead to a new discourse. Furthermore by activating stereotypes a mirror is created forcing observers to reflect on these unconscious assumptions of gendered role-expectations. Both ideas – namely breaking and strengthening stereotypes in order to provoke discussions can be realized in computer games. In other words, computer games could open up a space of political discussions on the existing dualistic gender concept and gender hierarchies.

FemCity[60]: A Gender-Inclusive Computer Game to Teach Feminism

Facing the problem that many young women doubt that gender discrimination exists, since in many cases they did not or even could not yet have experienced it, the Viennese Office of Women's Affairs[61] financed the development of a prototype of a computer game that simulates "being a woman" in a western industrialized city. The players are confronted with gendered life spheres such as education, art, jobs, family planning, and the like. So the goal was to make a gender-sensitive design and to teach feminism by using a game. This game, called FemCity, tries to incorporate results from research on gender and computer games. These results have been condensed by Agosto (2003) in two sets of guidelines which are based on female connotated interests:

Concerning girls' preferences in computer game content:
- Games that eschew the conflict between good and evil;
- Games that center on storylines and character development;
- Games that are not competitive in nature;
- Games that use real-life locales;
- Games that feature strong female characters who are in charge of decisions and actions;
- Games that enable users to play the role of main character, either through self-identification or through the power to make decisions;
- Games that focus on human relationships;
- Games with some educational value, as opposed to those designed purely for entertainment;
- Games containing nonviolent action;
- Games that reflect girls' common play patterns.

Concerning girls' preferences in computer game design:
- Games that enable them to play with other players, either online or in person (by sharing the same computer);
- Games with abundant high quality graphic and multimedia components;
- Games that enable online communication with other players during play.

---

60   The project team consisted of the following people: Edeltraud Hanappi-Egger, Vienna University of Economics and Business Administration: idea, concept, game specification and project leader; Gerhard Hanappi, Vienna University of Technology: game specification, economic expertise; Mathias Fuchs, Silvia Eckermann, University of Salford: visual and acoustic design. The prototype was developed in 2002-2004.

61   Frauenabteilung der Stadt Wien, www.magwien.gv.at/ma57/

Following these guidelines does not automatically lead to a game accepted by all, but it definitely is more inclusive than the "average" male-biased computer games focusing on a specific genre and leaving out any other game preferences.

FemCity follows these design principles and tries to open the game for a variety of player types. Furthermore, from the content point of view, the players are forced to reflect on role-expectations and self-understanding of being a woman. The game encourages players to make decisions and to learn about the consequences of these decisions within a social setting.

FemCity is a role playing game in multi-user mode. It was implemented in the Unreal Tournament Game Engine. At the beginning the gamers define their own aims along the lines of career/education and social relations by answering a questionnaire. The answers of nine questions are used to compute individual game objectives. Based on the activities in the game 'career indices' and 'social relation indices' are registered and finally assessed along the specified aims. So the players get a feedback concerning their gaming behavior in comparison with their a priori set objectives. The gaming time is set randomly symbolizing "real life expectations".

Figure 1:   The City

Various buildings in the city represent "topics" of the girls' lives such as education, jobs, relationships, family and the like (see figure 1). The buildings can be explored, general knowledge on women's issues can be discovered. Making decisions (e.g. leaving education) has consequences for other buildings (e.g. entering jobs), thus social causalities and structural interdependences are modeled.

FemCity can also be used to motivate girls to be interested in certain topics, such as gendered language, technical science and art, since the game consists of "knowledge spaces" inviting players to further investigate these topics. The technology and natural science room for example highlights the question "Who was the original goddess of earth in Greek mythology?" The answer "Gaia" is used as an introduction to the Gaia-Hypotheses, an interesting natural science concept of earth as self-organizing system.

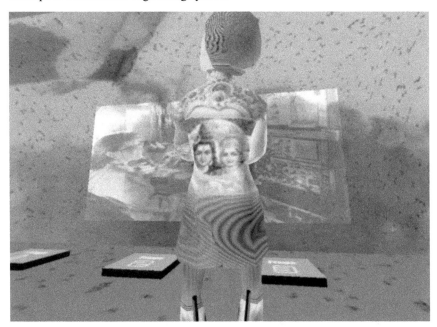

Figure 2:   The Natural Science and Technology Room

Generally speaking, the prototype of the game consists of several features offe-ring players (female as well as male) a wide range of debates on gender-related topics. Besides playing elements (dexterity in moving through the spaces), finding solutions (e.g. the necessity of getting an income without higher education) and making decisions (e.g. about partnerships) knowledge spaces are accessible. The players can read various boards in FemCity, or explore the library symbolized by huge books, to gain information on various topics. Furthermore the universities as well as the museum offer information and knowledge that could be discussed in more detail in follow-up activities with the players (e.g. in school projects).

Figure 3: entrance of university

Results of testing phase

As soon as a first version of the prototype of FemCity was ready, eight female test gamers with ages between 16 and 18 years (relatives of the department's staff) were invited to play and to reflect on the basic ideas and features of the game[62]. The players got a brief introduction and were observed while they were playing. A final discussion with the players ended the sessions.

---

62 Currently the game is being tested in several girls' communities in Vienna. The results are not yet available.

Concerning the *design* of the computer game the girls explicitly mentioned positively the quality of the graphics and the existence of the chatting feature allowing for communicating with the other players during the game. They enjoyed playing it in the multi-user mode allowing them to meet others in this virtual world.

Concerning the *content* of the game, the girls regarded FemCity as an interesting game and appreciated the real-life-locales. They liked to experiment and to explore the spaces. Additionally they used the chat function quite often in order to exchange knowledge on how to proceed in specific situations. Particularly interesting was the ongoing discussion about the content of the game. Spontaneous reactions like "Why am I responsible for childcare – where has the partner I have chosen gone?" or "S..., how can I get rid of the kids?" expressed irritation that could be used for subsequent discussions on gender-roles and their social implications.

Critiques mainly referred to the "model-like" appearance of the FemCity girls representing a specific kind of young woman, namely white, stylish and slim. The players also missed a more lively city atmosphere with other people and creatures, cars and other attractions. They also wondered why e.g. nutrition, violence and sport were no topics in FemCity[63].

The most interesting result of the test runs was that the players made many decisions without thinking them over carefully (e.g. no player read the texts concerning the choice of the pension system which the players have to make before entering the job building). In some cases it happened that the gamers "retired" without having enough money to consume goods. This was clearly a topic for later discussions about the underlying real-life situations. Similar dynamics developed with the causality of education and job opportunities or with family duties, partnerships and job opportunities.

As already mentioned, FemCity is just a prototype of a gender-sensitive computer game serving also to teach girls about emancipation issues and it could be much improved. Nevertheless, it shows that young women were interested in gaming and that they approached new media self-confidently. They enjoyed graphical quality as well as interactiveness and were willing to discuss gender topics. So it seems FemCity can contribute to the discussion on how to use games for social learning in terms of reflecting on gender-relations.

---

63   These topics had to be left out since the purpose of the project was to develop a limited
      prototype. The represented issues were the result of budget constraints.

Lessons Learned from FemCity

To follow gender-inclusive system guidelines in terms of design as well as content is an interesting but also ambivalent challenge. As mentioned earlier, the social construction of gender relations is manifested in technological artifacts such as computer games. Content, presentation and gaming context are socially shaped and consequently also gendered. However, consciously designing with gender sensitive guidelines is ambivalent in itself. On the one hand feminist computer system designers would argue that currently computer games serve men's playing preferences and leave out women's preferences. On the other side, this standpoint implies the identification of a common understanding of what "women's needs" are – and therefore it reproduces stereotypes.

The current discussion on how to encourage women to enter the field of engineering, by e.g. developing games, has to be questioned in the light of professional socialization. As Hanappi-Egger (2004b) argues, there are gendered dynamics such as "organizational sex" functioning as filter in the sense that the field of engineering and science sends gendered signs of masculinity and femininity. To be attracted by those signs means to follow specific gender patterns – independent of the biological sex the socially constructed gender leads to the fact that many female computer scientists have more in common with their male colleagues than with female social scientists. In other words, it is rather doubtful that female engineers – in particular after having experienced five to seven years mainstream education – should develop different software or develop it in a different way than men due to their biological constellation (see Paulitz, this book). It seems to be more promising to question the gender bias in the design and development processes themselves and to reflect on the role of the socially constructed images of the world. Besides individual biographical developments people are socialized in cultural and collective value systems, including gender dualism and gender hierarchies. With respect to this Allhutter and Hanappi-Egger (2005) showed that software designers and developers refer heavily to mental models of users and application contexts. They unconsciously embed personal perspectives and preferences into their products. This so-called "I-methodology" (Akrich 1995) would probably support the idea that women design software differently due to their socialization as a 'woman'. But as argued, only specific women enter the field of engineering, women who share many biographical elements with men. In addition, professional socialization influences the engineers' "I"-methodology. Engineers often believe to act in a gender-neutral way (and produce gender neutral products) but I would argue that they are gender-blind, because specific, masculine connotated, gender patterns are prioritized without them being aware of it. To go against this kind of design practices, means to focus on game contexts and preferences that attract a wider variety of players.

Breaking stereotypes, questioning genres and their content, widening the range of identification with game characters and offering a wider variety of game features would be the first steps.

The presented case of FemCity showed that gender-inclusive design aspects (such as multi-user mode, communication features, mixture of gaming elements such as puzzles, actions, and tasks for dexterity) and gender-inclusive content (such as real-life locales, eschewing the conflict between good and evil, female characters and the like) are appreciated by female players who are no intensive gamers.

Furthermore games are nice tools for learning about societal gender concepts. As FemCity showed the confrontation with gender-roles in the game lead to the fact that the girls were reflecting on the presented gendered spheres and tasks and started the discussion on mutual dependencies of gender and social chances, life quality and autonomy. Clearly there is still a lot of research on gender-inclusive system-design needed, but hopefully FemCity can serve as an example for the practical implications of theoretical gender-approaches.

References

Allhutter, Doris; Hanappi-Egger, Edeltraud (2005): Making the Invisible Visible: Mind-Scripting as Method of Deconstructing (IT-)System Design. In: Proceedings of the International Conference on Women in Engineering and Sciences (ICEWS), Seoul, Korea, 28.-30.August 2005.

Agosto, Denise E. (2003): Girls and Gaming: A Summary of the Research with Implications for Practice. Available: http://girlstech.douglass.rutgers.edu/gt_summary.html. Accessed November 2003.

Akrich, Madeleine (1995): User Representations: Practices, Methods and Sociology. In: Rip, Arie; Misa, Thomas J. and Schot, Johan (eds): Managing Technology in Society. The Approach of Constructive Technology Asssessment, London and New York: Pinter Publishers: 167-184.

Cassell, Justine; Jenkins, Henry (1998): Chess for girls? Feminism and Computer Games. In: Cassell, Justine; Jenkins, Henry (eds): From Barbie to Mortal Kombat: Gender and Computer Games: 2-45.

CESA (2002): Games White Paper. Tokyo, Computer Entertainment Software Association.

Douglas, Carol Anne; Dragiewicz, Molly; Manzano, Angie; McMullin, Vanessa (2002): United States: In video games, black women are victims, Latinas don't exist. In: Off Our Backs 43 (3-4): 6.

Gorriz, Cecilia M.; Medina, Claudia (2000): Engaging Girls with Computers through Software Games. In: Communications of the ACM 43: 42-49.

Hanappi-Egger, Edeltraud (2003): A Gendered View on New Technologies. In: Proceedings of the International Conference on Networking Entities, NETIES03, Cyprus.

Hanappi-Egger, Edeltraud (2004a): The Role of Gender in the Social Shaping of New Technology, 20th EGOS Colloquium, Ljubljana 1.-3. Juli 2004.

Hanappi-Egger, Edeltraud (2004b): Organisationsbezogene Ausschliessungsmechanismen von Frauen am Beispiel des technisch-naturwissenschaftlichen Bereiches. In: Schmidt, Angelika; Heitzmann, Karin (2004) (eds): Wege aus der Frauenarmut. Frankfurt am Main: Peter Lang Verlag.

Richard, Birgit (2003): Grrls who got game: Die Konstruktion von weiblichen Repräsentationsbildern in Computerspielen. Research-report. Available: www.birgitrichard.de. Accessed November 2003.

Wajcman, Judy (2001): The Built Environment, Women's Place, Gendered Space. In: Wyer, Mary; Barbercheck, Mary; Giesman, Donna; Öztürk Hatice Ö.; Wayne, Marta (eds): Women, Science, and Technology. London: Routledge: 194-208.

Weber, Barbara (2004): Frauen im Computerspielmarkt. Eine Analyse der Spielfiguren und Rollenbilder, sowie des Einflusses der weiblichen Entwicklerinnen auf die Inhalte und das Design von Computerspielen, Master's Thesis at the Department of „Gender and Diversity in Organizations", Vienna University of Economics and Business Administration.

Logogo – An Approach to the Design of Girl-Specific Educational Software

Bettina Munk

Most western countries report a lack of female computer science students. Women are highly underrepresented in technology careers and in technology-related decision-making positions. This problem is currently much discussed, and solutions for providing girls with equal opportunities for education and career choices are looked for.

One idea to raise girls' interest in technology is to extend their experience with technology that suits their interests and needs and thereby raise their technology competencies. I assume that gender-specific software that is based on girls' media and computing interests could help girls and young women to find their own way into computing. For this purpose, the idea emerged to develop software that relates to the specific interests of teenage girls and offers them a platform to gain basic insights into programming. This article describes the analyses of girls' media interests and the construction and purpose of the designed software LogoGo.

This article examines and analyzes previous research on gender differences in the use of media and computer technology and discusses the findings. Subsequently the intentions, emergence, focus, and structure of LogoGo as educational software are demonstrated, and conclusions for the construction and use of gender-specific software are presented.

1 Computing and Media Interests of Girls and Young Women

Looking for an answer to the question, how gender specific software relating to girls' interests could help girls and young women to find their own way into computing, this section turns to the findings of research on gender differences in the use of media and computer technology. First it highlights the situation of young women in computer science and examines two reports from American universities. It then analyzes German studies on juvenile interest in media and computers.

2.2 Women in Computer Science

Most western countries report a lack of female computer science (CS) students: In Germany females continuously represent between 14 and 20 percent of all CS students (Statistisches Bundesamt 2005). According to the US National Science Foundation (2003) women earned less than 27 % of bachelor's degrees in computer science in 1998, with percentages falling between 1990 and1998. Since many international studies address this phenomenon without definitive answers, we would like to discuss some interesting, and at times divergent, conclusions offered by two studies from US colleges.

Greg Scragg and Jesse Smith from SUNY Geneseo State University of New York conducted a study about barriers to women in undergraduate computer science (Scragg, Smith 1998). They asked why so few women complete a computer science major. A questionnaire with a combination of the most frequent comments from the focus groups and on hypotheses from the literature that seemed most plausible was filled out by a group of introductory computer science students at SUNY Geneseo.

Within this group, they found no evidence of peer, parental, or personal perceptions that computer science is a career inappropriate for women. Nor did their study yield significant differences that might explain why women do not stay in the field. Their final conclusion was that the largest barriers to retaining women in computer science may be circumstances that occur long before women enter the programs: They have had far less experience with computing and did not intend to continue the major. Scragg and Smith suggested it was a problem of recruitment or outreach, and hoped for programs awakening girls' interest in computing.

Jane Margolis and Allan Fisher together with Faye Miller published several papers (1998, 1999) in which they came to more in-depth conclusions after following more than 100 computer science students, both male and female, at Carnegie Mellon University for four years beginning in 1995. They found a definitive difference in attitude towards computers expressed by male and female first-year computer science students.

They asked students to tell the story of themselves and computers. Male students frequently responded that they were consumed with computing from an early age, that their view was often proprietary: the fun of the computer is not only in using it, but in knowing it. Females, however, described an "outsider" position with respect to the machine. They related their interest in computing to other arenas, to a social context that is more people-oriented. This confirms Sherry Turkle's observation that mastery is one of the essences of male hacker culture:

"Most hackers are young men for whom at a very early age mastery became highly charged, emotional, colored by a particular desire for perfection, and focused on triumph over things. Their pleasure is in manipulating and mastering their chosen object, in proving themselves with it." (Turkle 1984: 201)

These appetites contrast with women students' pleasure in programming as problem-solving. Margolis et al. (1998) find that many women enjoy computing when it is "computing for a purpose".

Furthermore Margolis et al. describe the effects of the males' stereotyped view on CS culture as being one of myopically-focused hackers. Male students who felt they did not conform to this image did not seem to be much affected or distressed by the perceived gap. Female students, however, felt distress about the perceived lack of fit between themselves and the prevailing notion of what a computer science student was supposed to be, they felt inadequate and deficient. This brings the researchers to the following conclusion:

"If the computer science culture can let women know that they can succeed without knowing everything about computing before entering college, and without adopting a stereotyped obsessive persona, it will have taken a step forward creating a more diverse population of computer science students and professionals." (ibid.)

1.2 Teenagers' Media Usage

Girls still seem to have less hands-on experience in computing than boys. How come girls do not care more about getting practice in computing with all the digital gadgets so common in their everyday life? To answer this question we want to focus in-depth on teenage girls and their overall involvement in different media.

Since 1998, an annual survey in Germany has been collecting data about teenagers' exposure to TV, computer, radio, books, and cellular phones (Medienpädagogischer Forschungsverbund Südwest 2004, 2005): The "Jugend, Information, (Multi-)Media" studies (Youth, Information, (Multi-) Media, JIM-study in the following) are based on telephone interviews with around 1000 teenagers aged 12-19.

Overall, TV is the teenagers' favorite medium. While girls and young women fancy daily soaps, mysteries and series, boys and young men prefer sports and news. As in earlier years, the surveys show differences in the teenagers' approach to media. While boys spend their time involved with computers and the Internet, girls' interests spread a field toward auditive media and books, and an intense use of cell phones.

1.2.1   Girls and Cellular Phones

90% of all teenagers use cell phones. However, girls lead the statistics over boys by a few percent. Sending an SMS (text message) is the most important feature in cell phones used by teenagers under 16, and again girls show more activity with this than boys. One of the main attractions of text messaging to the teenage crowd is that it is inexpensive. There is little reliable data on teenagers sending MMS[64]. Granted that this service cheapens the price, similar frequencies may be found for sending MMS in the future.

Another study conducted with 949 female and 922 male teenagers and young adults from the German Rheinland (Nowotny 2003) points out that girls love sending SMS and have collections of incoming "dear messages". Girls use cell phones to connect with friends; they seek comfort in the use of this technology.

1.2.2   Girls and Computers

While computers recently became a more available tool in German schools and homes, girls make use of it in a far more practical and less passionate way than boys. Girls use the computer mainly as a writing tool. They also use it for creative issues like painting and drawing. On the Internet, the girls' main activity is sending e-mails and visiting chat rooms. They exhibit far less interest in random surfing than boys. The 2004 JIM-study finds a difference between girls and boys in frequently using a computer together with teachers in school. Girls do so at a far lower level. The study suggests that it has to do with the fact that far more boys than girls are active in so called "Computer AGs" (computer clubs), voluntarily attended courses with teachers to learn about computers (Medienpädagogischer Forschungsverbund Südwest 2004: 49). "Programming" as a frequent activity was answered positively by 10 % of the boys compared to 3 % of the girls.

The AAUW Educational Foundation (2000) report finds that many girls state: "We can, but we don't want to". It lists a lack of choices in technology as one of their main reasons for disengagement in school-based technology activities.

---

64   MMS: Multiple Media Service – enables the sending of pictures together with a short message

1.2.3   Girls and Computer Games

There is a big gap between girls and boys when it comes to their respective interest in computer games. Playing computer games is the number one activity of boys on the computer offline, compared to only a fraction of girls' activity. This still might have its cause in the contents of computer games. Graner Ray (2004) points to the martial design and content of computer games in general, and Schindler (1993) describes the appalling, limited and boring roles of female characters.

Different approaches to challenges faced by girls or boys might also play a role in their respective attraction to computer games. Many girls tend to analyze a situation completely before solving a problem, while boys prefer the strategy of trial and error (Dittler 1995). Girls prefer strategy- and brainteaser-games (Medienpädagogischer Forschungsverbund Südwest 2004:11).

Up until recently, most electronic game companies marketed mostly to boys. However, things are changing. Mattel Media, Her Interactive, Girl Games, Inc., and Girl Tech are four software companies that offer a product line specifically geared toward girls.

Furthermore on websites like www.girltech.com the statement reads that products for girls aged 8-12 "are designed with girls' play preferences in mind, addressing issues that are important to them such as privacy and communication". Many of these companies have sponsored research studies and focus groups to discover exactly what appeals to girls in electronic games. They found that girls enjoy identifying with the characters, would rather create than destroy something, and that they like to win through collaborative rather than competitive methods (Inkpen et al. 1995).

1.2.4   Creativity and Computer Savviness

Girls and young women fancy creative activities more than their male peers. From an early age their creativity is often expressed through communication. They write letters or text messages to friends and expect these to be collected and preserved. Their pleasure in narratives and in identifying with characters extends to computer games. Moreover, the surveys show girls love to be involved in creative activities that require technical skills.

Concerning the practical experience of adolescents in media design, the JIM-studies report a distinctive activity of teenage girls in the field of video and audio editing, in creating radio drama or designing a newspaper. A striking number of teenage girls and young women articulate a more intense desire for independent and active engagement with all kinds of media than boys and young men. This includes the desire to design a website (Medienpädagogischer Forschungsverbund Südwest 2004: 60).

The studies about media use of teenagers reveal some differences in general: girls and young women fancy creative activities like drawing, painting and writing letters and postcards more than their male peers (Medienpädagogischer Forschungsverbund Südwest 2004 and 2005).

As adults, young women with an interest in computing tend to switch to applied computer science focusing on media instead of engaging in computer science itself (Fröhlich, Schwenk 2004).

1.3 Discussion of the Findings

Most findings only highlight the difference between female and male approach towards media and computers. Empirical studies tend to use a short cut to analyze the situation, and do not take into account the circumstances in the education of girls and female teenagers.

The cited findings of Scragg & Smith and of Margolis et al. state that girls who want to major in computer science and enroll in a computer science program actually enter with less hands-on experience. Although there was no difference in ability, there was a difference in experience, which then led to a difference in self-confidence during the study program. Margolis et al. found that female computer science students are interested in programming as problem-solving. Unfortunately, the academic curriculum and the reward system still do not account for the female students' approach to computer science as "computing for a purpose", and especially in early courses, instruction often focuses primarily on technical concerns.

The 2004 JIM-study only reports that girls attend computer clubs less often than boys. Additionally, it reports that girls are quite open and interested in using computers as media for creative activities. This obvious contradiction may perhaps be explained by the gap between girls' desires and the current styles of technical education offered.

In general, computing is still considered to be a boys' territory and not so much a typical girls' interest. Many girls apparently endorse the stereotype of computers as predominantly boys' tools, and see a computer as a medium that can only be mastered technically. And technical mastery of computing is often related to the hacker culture. As long as computing is continuously noted as the domain of a hacker minded persona, girls are put off much more than boys.

"Hacking is a purely male domain, and in that sense a clearly gendered space." (Sollfrank 1999: 41)

The girls' resulting perceptions may be something like that: If computing is hacking, and hacking is for boys, then computing is not interesting for me. Therefore, the idea was born to offer girls a computing experience that meets their interests.

2   The Development of LogoGo

Based on the research quoted above about women's smaller amount of technical experience before entering computer science, their interest in working on meaningful projects and doing computing "for a purpose", and about the different interests and uses of girls and boys regarding media and computers, we suggest that educational software directed at girls' interests could be a way to raise girls' interest and experience in programming and computing. The idea for designing LogoGo was born.

At first, LogoGo was a project by three female design students and their woman tutor in a course on how to program in Flash for web design at the FHTW University of Applied Sciences, Berlin. We met additionally to voluntarily extend the course beyond what the curriculum had arranged for design students. From these meetings, the idea emerged to develop software that offers teenage girls a platform to learn programming. Despite the difference in age and heritage (i.e. West or East Germany) all participants in the project shared a common experience, having been a female teenager with less practice, interest, and confidence in their ability toward computing compared to their male peers.

We designed the software while keeping in mind the idea of learning computing "for a purpose". LogoGo offers girls an approach to computing that relates to their media interests without patronizing them. Our approach to teaching explicitly considers the interests of girls and young females in a specific period of their adolescence.

Research studies as quoted suggest that girls show different preferences from boys toward learning systems, and there we find that the school system as part of a social system structurally serves boys' interests better than girls' regarding the field of teaching technical skills like computing. Our objective was to design gender-specific educational software that meets girls' use and interests in media and computing in order to direct them to understand programming.

2.1 Idea and Functionality of LogoGo

The intention of LogoGo is to create a positive image and understanding of computing that is different to the perceived hacking image.

LogoGo is educational software focusing on learning competence, not subject-matter mastery. It was particularly designed to avoid discouragement by allowing the user to gain immediate satisfying results without an emphasis on technical mastery. The educational software offers progressive insights into the field of programming. The young users attain more competence in recognizing programming as a set of rules for a potential space of content that they can create on their own. We kept in mind the specific resourcefulness of girls and young women by encouraging them to work on their technical achievements with creativity: taking into account girls' specific interests, we intended to fill rules and functions to be learned with "life", so they would serve an obvious purpose and thereby can be understood and used successfully.

The software LogoGo is geared toward teenagers, particularly girls, aged 10 to 17. The software's hands-on structure is customized to the preferences of this age group, focusing on their actual media activities and communication. Girls' interests and intentions as shown above are to write and send messages, be creative, exchange music, pictures, and video clips, etc. And this is what they can do with LogoGo.

Teenagers install the software LogoGo on their computer, then collect their favorite images and sound files in several folders organized by a database.

The "Link Girl" shows up as the main character, it can be designed according to the user's interests: She can give her a name, put her in a certain environment, dress her, design a backpack for her and fill her backpack with music, pictures, etc.

The educational goal of LogoGo is to point to the programming code necessary for such alterations and developments. Therefore it provides explanations on what to do next and visibly displays programming code for each step. Also it makes suggestions for which code to use. The Link Girl explains all processes and helps to proceed. The processes are performed in several toolboxes integrated into one window. Accordingly, users always see all processes on the screen, both the programming and the results.

Additionally, users can create a movie clip and send it out to their friends' cell phones or e-mail addresses. During the process of design, the young users understand that a code lies behind the images and animations in the Internet and on the cell phone, and that their first choices in pop music, idols, fashion and animations are integrated into the abstract process of programming as their favorite images and sounds are animated by the code.

Figure 1:   LogoGo main area displaying four toolboxes

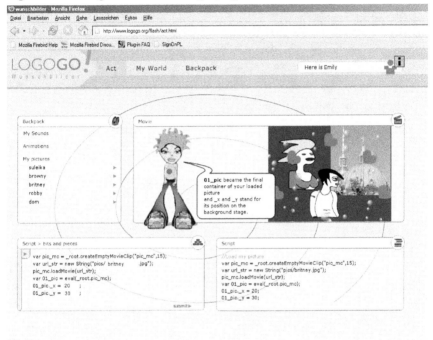

By filling individual information into the white fields, the programming code is altered. From the toolbox "Script > bits and pieces" (lower left) the users choose the right code module for their task and connect it to their favorite images, sounds and animations, organized in the „backpack", the database of the software. They watch their world of pictures and sounds in the window 'Movie' being animated by code displayed in the 'Script' window.

The Link Girl is a central element, intended to communicate the concept of programming during the process. It can be accessed in the menu (see picture 2). LogoGo has three central activities: They are called "Act", "My World", and "Backpack". The Link Girl can be personalized to the girls' own tastes; it can be dressed, named and redesigned in the LogoGo section "My World".

Figure 2:   Logogo window with Link Girl

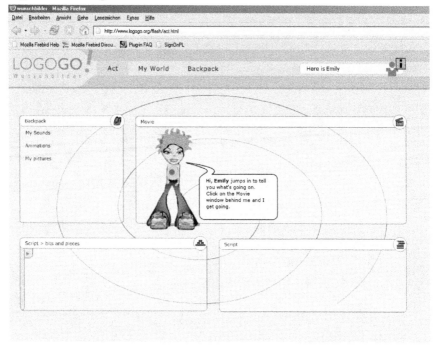

Another feature in the software is a link to an associated website, where users can get new elements like Link Girl outfits and wallpaper images to customize their tool, and a chat room.

Intentionally LogoGo does not use a simplified programming language as a circuitous route to learning how to program. It rather offers a programming language with a real-time result during the process of teaching. The barrier to understanding is not a scripting language's complexity itself but the way of imparting its complexity. The programming of a movie clip to be sent as MMS or e-mail can be done on different levels. Beginner level allows sending out a message without the need for special knowledge in computing.

From the start the user gets a good impression of what is characteristic about a scripting language functioning behind the imagery. On the next level, she can create more complex movie clips by writing and editing the code herself. During the creation and design phase of the clip, the software always keeps the code visible. Without pressure, LogoGo offers progressive possibilities to learn programming. Step by step, higher levels challenge the computer savvy girl to become her best.

2.2   The Basis of LogoGo: Connecting to Girls' Media Interests

2.2.1   LogoGo is a tool for sending a MMS or e-mail to a friend

For teenagers the cell phone means more than a communication medium to make phone calls: it influences their everyday habits and their attitude. As Höflich (2001) found, it is a very personal medium.

As the JIM-studies also stated, young teenage girls basically have a positive attitude towards writing letters and postcards in their leisure time. Thus, staying in touch with their friends is important. Therefore supporting the girls' preferences in the first place, LogoGo dismantles their reservation towards the use of computing resources. Even in utilizing the software as a simple tool, the user has a satisfying result with the side effect of getting an impression of how programming works.

2.2.2   LogoGo's Ambience

The JIM-study reveals girls' ample preoccupation with "daily soaps". In her survey Jeannine Simon (2004) states that, without girls, the TV soap operas would not exist. The interviewed girls indicated that their intention to continually watch daily soap operas was curiosity in the narrative and an emotional identification with the persona of some actors. Soap operas are designed as endless sagas. Young girls even watch these episodes to look out for new trends.

The affinity of young girls to identify with and then personalize a character is reflected by the helping feature in the software LogoGo: the 'Link Girl'. The Link Girl can be customized, dressed, and redesigned. Our intention is to make young users feel comfortable. The software also reflects the girls' desire for communication by offering an associated website to chat, upload and download new Link Girl outfits and wallpaper to customize their tool. This website is the place for girls to show their own Link Girl creation or their movie clips to a wider audience.

3 Concluding Remarks

This article has examined and analyzed existing research on the difference between female and male teenagers' and computer science students' approaches towards media and computers. It concluded that in the paramount reality of the school and university systems, the computing education does not consider the desires and interests of girls and young women. The gap revealed between the interest in technical media expressed by girls and young women and their actual activity in dealing with computers must be addressed, for it mainly stems from an early misjudgement of computing, as well as a discomfort with the learning environment.

One step into the direction of change could be a renewed IT-design that focuses on girls' particular creativity and their interest in becoming creative. The development of new gender-specific software for almost every sphere of media activity could be geared towards girls at an early age. Differentiated educational software could invite them to new ways of engaging in their creative process, and could influence their mindset later in life. In this sense, gender-specific software would help to take charge of the deplorable state of affairs, rather than discriminate against the other gender.

The design, intention, and functionality of LogoGo were described as an example for educational software geared at girls' media interests.

4 Acknowledgments

From the year 2005 on, LogoGo is developed and promoted by Yvonne Prätzel in partnership with Bettina Munk and was presented as a prototype in the exhibition "Coolhunters" at the ZKM, the centre for art and media / Karlsruhe, in May 2005. For further information see: www.logogo.org

References

The American Association of University Women (AAUW) (ed.) (2000): Tech-Savvy: Educating Girls in the New Computer Age. Washington, DC: AAUW Educational Foundation Research.
Bendig, Daria (2001): Computerkids zwischen Bildschirmspielen und Lernsoftware. Dortmund: Fachhochschule Dortmund FB Sozialpädagogik, Unpublished Diploma Thesis. Dortmund.

Dittler, Ullrich (1995): Frauen und Computerspiele (Teil 1) – Geschlechtsspezifische Unterschiede im Umgang mit Video- und Computerspielen. Jugend-Medien-Schutz-Report 3/95. Baden-Baden: Nomos-Verlag.

Fröhlich, Romy; Schwenk, Johanna (2004): Traumberuf Medien? Daten und Fakten zu einem vermeintlich frauendominierten Berufsfeld. Wiesbaden: VS Verlag.

Graner Ray, Sheri (2004): Gender Inclusive Game Design: Expanding the Market. Hingham/Mass.: Charles River Media Inc.

Howell, Kathy (1993): The Experience of Women in Undergraduate Computer Science: What does the Research Say? In: SIGCE Bulletin 25 (2): 1-8.

Höflich, Joachim R. (2001): Das Handy als persönliches Medium. Zur Aneignung des Short Message Service (SMS) durch Jugendliche. In: kommunikation@gesellschaft 2 (1) Available: http://www.soz.uni-frankfurt.de/K.G/B1_2001_Hoeflich.pdf (Last accessed: 2006-04-28).

Inkpen, Kori; Booth, Kellogg; Klawe, Maria; Upitis, Rena (1995): Playing together beats playing apart, especially for girls. In: Proceedings of Computer Supported Collaborative Learning (CSCL) '95 Mahwah, NJ: Lawrence Erlbaum Associates: 177-181.

Klawe, Maria; Leveson, Nancy (1990): Women in Computing: Where Are We Now? In: Communications of the ACM 38 (1): 29-35.

Liu, Mei-Ling; Blanc, Lori (1996): On the Retention of Female Computer Science Students. In: Proceedings of the Twenty Seventh SIGCSE Technical Symposium on Computer Science Education: 32–36.

Margolis, Jane; Fisher, Allan; Miller, Faye (1998): Caring About Connections: Gender and Computing In: IEEE Technology and Society 18 (4): 13-20.

Margolis, Jane; Fisher, Allan (2002): Unlocking the Clubhouse: Women in Computing. Cambridge/Mass: MIT Press.

Medienpädagogischer Forschungsverbund Südwest (2004): JIM-Studie: Jugend, Information, (Multi-)Media ; Basisstudie zum Medienumgang 12- bis 19jähriger. Baden-Baden: MPFS. Available at: http://www.mpfs.de/studien/jim/Brosch%FCre%20JIM %2004.pdf (Last accessed: 2006-04-28).

Medienpädagogischer Forschungsverbund Südwest (2005): JIM-Studie: Jugend, Information, (Multi-)Media ; Basisstudie zum Medienumgang 12- bis 19jähriger. Baden-Baden: MPFS. Available at: http://www.mpfs.de/studien/jim/JIM-Studie2005.pdf (Last accessed: 2006-04-28).

National Science Foundation (2003): Women, minorities and persons with disabilities in science and engineering: 2002. Available at: http://www.nsf.gov/statistics/nsf03312/ pdfstart.htm (last accessed 2006-05-05).

Nowotny, Andrea (2004): Daumenbotschaften. Zur Bedeutung von Handy und SMS für Jugendliche im Rheinland. Landschaftsverband Rheinland, Amt für rheinische Landeskunde Bonn. Bonn. Available at: http://www.lvr.de/FachDez/Kultur/Landeskunde/Alltagskultur/kompetenz/Volkskunde/projekte/daumenbotschaften.pdf (Last accessed: 2006-05-05).

Pearl, Amy; Pollack, Martha E.; Riskin, Eve; Thomas, Becky; Wolf, Elizabeth; Wu, Alice (1990): Becoming a Computer Scientist. In: Communications of the ACM 33 (11): 47–57.

Schindler, Friedemann (1993): Computerspiele in der Hand von Kindern und Jugendlichen. Eine Untersuchung über die Verbreitung und den Stellenwert problematischer Computerspiele. In: Bundeszentrale für politische Bildung (ed.): Computerspiele: Bunte Welt im grauen Alltag - ein medien- und kulturpädagogisches Arbeitsbuch. Bonn: Bundeszentrale für Politische Bildung: 105-112.

Simon, Jeannine (2004): Wirkungen von Daily Soaps auf Jugendliche. München: Verlag Reinhard Fischer.

Scragg, Greg; Smith, Jesse (1998): A Study of Barriers to Women in Undergraduate Computer Science. In: ACM SIGCSE Bulletin 30 (1): 82-86.

Sollfrank, Cornelia (1999): Woman Hackers. In: Old boys network (ed.): Next Cyberfeminist International, Berlin: Verlag b_books: 41-45.

Statistisches Bundesamt (2005): Schnellmeldungsergebnisse der Hochschulstatistik. Available at: http://www.destatis.de/presse/deutsch/pk/2005/aktuelle_ergebnisse.pdf (Last accessed: 2006-05-05).

Turkle, Sherry (1984): The Second Self: Computers and the Human Spirit. New York: Simon and Schuster.

Robotics and Gender: The Use of Robotics for the Empowerment of Girls in the Classroom

Susann Hartmann, Heike Wiesner, Andreas Wiesner-Steiner

0   Introduction

It is difficult to foster students' enthusiasm about technical topics in conventional ways. Therefore, high dropout rates of over 50% and steadily dropping numbers of beginners in the engineering disciplines are the consequence. Only few women study these subjects. A report by the American Educational Foundation (AAUW 2000), states that women often argue "we can but we don't want to". As Seymour Papert has put it, the technical curiosity thus needs to be established somehow behind people's backs (Papert 1994). The fascination of robotics combined with multi-media learning might offer an innovative attempt. But is robotics suited to raise girls' and women's interest in technology?

Our article presents results from the evaluation of robotics courses using Lego Mindstorms that aim at the empowerment of young women in shaping technology. These courses were designed and performed within the project Roberta[65] and have been evaluated through the help of questionnaires, interviews and video analysis. The project's basic assumption is that the activity of robot construction offers possibilities to develop more self-confidence in one's skills and thus provide an attractive access to technology for girls. The first section of this article pays particular attention to the impact of the courses on students' self-concepts and their orientation towards computer science and technology, whereas the second section discusses how didactics and technology interact and how the materiality of robotics itself plays an important role here i.e., the fact that it already comes along as gendered material. Due to that, we suggest a new gender-oriented approach towards the use of robotics in education. If carefully

---

65   „Roberta – girls conquer robotics" was funded by the German Federal Ministry of Education and Research (BMBF) and launched by the Fraunhofer Institute (AIS) (Müllerburg et al. 2004). It was scientifically accompanied by the University of Bremen, Digitale Media in Education (DiMeB) and the Institute for Didactics of Natural Sciences (IDN). Roberta addresses 10 – 16 year old girls.

used, robotics not only suit boys' and girls' interests in technology but enables them to prepare for an active role in a technologically mediated life.

1   The Practice of Robotics Courses

Lego robot construction kits consist of complementary mechanical, dynamic and electronic parts that allow the construction and programming of different types of robots. Basic models can be equipped with different engines and sensors (contact sensors and optical sensors). The programming can be done in two programming languages (RIS and NQC). The programmes are transmitted onto the RCX module, a programmable Lego brick with 3 input sockets for sensors and 3 for engines. In a typical 2-4 hour-long Roberta course the students often start with the construction of a small robot. Many courses provide students with a basic robot that only needs additional construction. Some courses however let students build the whole robot from scratch. After this construction phase, a short introduction into programming follows, often including small exercises that help to build up the skills required to solve the course's programming task. Programming aims vary: some courses work with treasure hunts in which the robots have to avoid barriers in order to get to a treasure. Other courses' tasks are to move through a maze or program the robots not to cross lines in order to have them imprisoned in a circle. At the end of a course the students present their robot by performing the planned activity (e.g. reaching the treasure). Courses use the Lego Software RIS for its simplicity as the courses address beginners. In longer courses from 6 to up to 20 hours, NQC and other programming languages are used.

The findings we present in this article are thus focused on the following questions:
- How can the interest of girls and women in technology be aroused by the use of robotics?
- Is robotics a suitable activity to influence student's self-esteem and influence their orientations towards technology?
- Which didactical concept is appropriate in connection with robotics?
- How should learning environments be designed in order to satisfy both girls and boys?

Picture 1:   Constructing robots

2   Evaluation Design and Data Basis

Our evaluation is based on a quantitative as well as on a qualitative approach. Both approaches were developed and carried out at the University of Bremen (DiMeB and IDN).[66] In the quantitative approach we evaluated every course while the qualitative approach chose specific courses in order to explore their structure and effects in more detail. The quantitative data are based on answers of about 500 students (425 girls and 74 boys) who participated in Roberta courses.[67] Courses took

---

66   In a first step the initiators of Roberta were interviewed in order to find out their project aims. Secondly a questionnaire for the course tutors (students, school teachers, museum teams) was designed in order to find out whether the aims of the course tutors were in accordance with the aims of the project initiators. Furthermore this questionnaire helped to get information about the courses. It was split into two parts, the first one was answered before and the second one after each course.

67   The students' questionnaires allow a comparison of students' self-confidence before and after a course. These questionnaires also include questions concerning students' prior experiences, their motivation to sign up for a course, their thoughts on future career options, their con-

place both in school and outside school settings (e.g. museums, girls' days at universities). Each course lasted at least two but not more than four hours. Most students were between 11 and 16 years old.

The qualitative data have an explorative character and are based on (group-) interviews with robotics experts, tutors and students as well as video analysis of several courses that differed in length and setting.[68] So far, four Roberta courses (2-8 hour-courses) have been qualitatively evaluated. In this paper we will present results from both approaches, starting with quantitative results.

3   Empowerment through Influence on Student Confidence and Orientation

Roberta courses are well liked by students, 94% of 499 participants think the courses are fun. There is no gender difference in the answers to this question, but the number rises to 98% for those 205 students who took part in courses whose tutors say that they put a special effort into gender-awareness. 94% of these 205 students would advise a friend to take part in such a course while this is true for 88% of all participants.

As these results show the courses are well liked by participants, but why? Students' answers in the questionnaires give some interesting hints. In an open question many students write that they liked the freedom to realize their own ideas and enjoyed constructing and programming. We believe that the mixture of freedom and guidance is very much responsible for the success of the courses. In a closed question 75% of the 423 girls agree to the statement "I could realize my own ideas", while this statement is true for 65% of the boys.

Apart from this, students also state that they have learned something in the courses. Girls (88%) and boys (87%) state that they learned how to program a robot and 75% of the girls as well as 80% of the boys feel that they have learned how to construct a robot. The difference between the two items is no surprise, as students and tutors agree upon the fact that the emphasis of the courses lay in programming more than constructing. Furthermore over 80% of all participants think that they have learned something about tasks robots can master.

In order to find out with what prior knowledge students come to the courses we asked them to rank different activities. Even though the questionnaire we used is not as elaborate, our findings are similar to an international study conducted by Sjoberg (2002). As shown in table 1, girls who participated in

---

tentment with the course and the presumed learning effects.
68   For the design of the qualitative method see: Wiesner 2004, p. 128-132.

Roberta courses state to have less prior experience with activities like "programming", "installing software" or "talking with friends about computers".[69]

I have already often...	girls	boys
talked about computers with friends	34%	67%
installed software	37%	66%
dealt with robotics	32%	59%
programmed	16%	37%
read about how machines work	55%	56%

Table 1: Students' agreement to some of the questions concerning prior knowledge N=499 (425 girls, 74 boys)

These findings are illuminating especially when we assume that experiences are the basis for self-confidence, and if we consider self-confidence to be essential for future interests and future career choice. Differences between boys and girls also might have to do with the girls' understatement. As we did not test the prior knowledge with tasks or activities, all we have is the estimation of the participants. Our motivation in asking this question was to find out, whether students with more or less prior experiences enjoyed the courses more or less. However, results show no influence of prior knowledge. Courses are well liked by students independent of their prior knowledge. This is astonishing and may be explained by the mixture of free and ordered structure most courses have. It is possible that since all students can choose challenges that match their abilities nobody feels unhappy because the course is too easy or too difficult for them.

Are students more confident concerning their abilities in science and technology after they participated in a course? Do perspectives on future jobs or school careers change?

Results show an impact of the courses on students' confidence as well as students' orientation towards a professional development in the area of computer science and technology. In the questionnaire seven items are related to confiden-

---

69   Sjoberg (2002) reports results from a study in which 10000 thirteen years old in 21 countries were asked about their experiences and interests related to science and technology. Sjoberg finds that girls compared to boys have less out-of-school experiences with technology and science related activities. This tendency is true for 80 activities that students were asked about in the questionnaire. "Electricity-related experiences are strongly male-dominated in all countries. In some countries, boys seem to have twice as much experiences in this field than the girls. (...) It may be a surprise that boys in even the poorest countries have more experience with electricity than girls in industrialized countries." (Sjoberg 2002, p. 6)

ce and orientation. The reliability is with Conbach's alpha 0,75 for confidence and 0,83 for orientation satisfactory. This means that the items of each scale fit together and don't load on different scales.

Students' answers before a course were compared to students' answers after a course using the Wilcoxon test (Bühl, Zöfel 2004). Items for development of confidence are for example: "When others talk about technology I have nothing to say." or "When I make an effort I can be good at science." Items for orientation were for example: "I would like to have more lessons at school that deal with technology." or "I might chose a profession that deals with technology later on."

A factor analysis shows that students' answers can be divided into subscales. For orientation these subscales can be labelled "now at school" and "later when I work," while for confidence the subscales are divided by the subjects "computer science" and "natural science" (the technology items load on both subscales).

Students express higher confidence in their computer related abilities after attending a course. The significance of this change is p=0.005 for the scale with all seven items. For single items the significance is with p=0.000 even higher yet the effect size even for the items with very high significance in the changes in students' answers is not higher than d=0.29. Therefore we can speak of highly significant changes but small effects. Nevertheless this is an astonishingly good result for courses that last only 2 to 4 hours.

The effect is higher for students who attend courses in which tutors expressed that they put a special effort to gender awareness (for some items d=0.4). Figure 1 illustrates the change in students' answers for one item of the self-confidence scale.

"If I wanted to, I could become an expert in computer science"

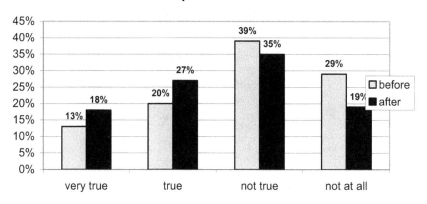

Figure 1:   Students' answers before and after attending a Roberta course.
N=499, p=0,000, d=0,29

While the change in students' answers concerning the orientation subscale "later when I work" are highly significant (p=0.000) this is not true for the subscale "now at school". Students distinguish between now and later and while the courses have positive influence on what they imagine to become later there is no difference in answers concerning the present school situation. Nobody knows which professions students are going to choose later on in life, and it might be easier to dream about the future than to imagine a change of the present situation. Nevertheless it is remarkable that students' answers change at all. The direction of the chance for the subscale "later when I work" is intended and shows high significance but has a very small effect size. Students' answers to one item of this subscale shall be looked at more closely. After attending Roberta courses students are more likely to imagine studying computer science when they are older. Yet most students (62%) still think studying computer science is nothing they want to do. Students' answers to this item are illustrated in figure 2.[70]

---

70   For a more detailed description of the quantitative results see Hartmann, Schecker 2005.

"One day I might study computer science"

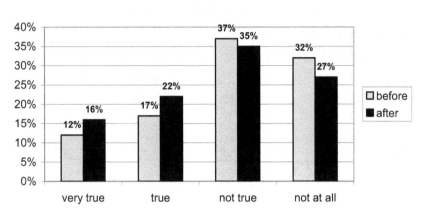

Figure 2:   Students' answers before and after attending a Roberta course.
                 N=499, p=0,000, d=0,12

4   The Didactical Treatment of Gendered Material: "...the boys' ideas were dominating and they all centered round wheels"

The quantitative results clearly demonstrate a positive impact of the courses. In addition, qualitative results suggest that these positive effects result from the didactical conception of the courses. An open and creative robotics course concept is the basic precondition for an understanding of technological processes. To promote interest and self-confidence, it seems to be important to enable learning processes instead of steering them, to open learning paths instead of installing fixed routines. The technology being used, whether as hardware or software, must be transparent and ought to enable children to develop and experiment with their own solutions. This aspect can easily be elaborated by the qualitative evaluation. A tutor says: "It is an incentive, not just to program, but to program something to do something..." The children are enthusiastic and when they first encounter the robot construction set, the instructions from the tutors do not reach them anymore, simply because they immediately have their hands on something. This has been described by a tutor:

> "[...] it's really an adventure to handle all these modules, to unpack them, fit the engines, there is something turning. [...] You can do so much with the set, there are

700 nice little colored parts, from eyes to hats and the gearwheels are also exciting […] One can also put things in action with the sets, because five programs are already preinstalled on the yellow module. As soon as the batteries are in and students start moving with program 1 – one can attach the sensors and with program 2 the engine turns […] This has convinced me to use the sets. You need not do much, you can use it in class without any preparation at all, I'd say." (translation by H.W.)

Right from the start the material speaks for itself, because the children handle something they already know. The programmable bricks, engines, and sensors, however, provide an unknown means to make experiences, so that children of both sexes are usually confronted with something new, too. Like computers, the Lego material in this sense is evocative (Turkle 1984) i.e. it generates presumptions, experiences and actions by itself. In addition, it even appears to be "gendered material". The use of a car-like basic model for example often leads to car-like robots.

Picture 2:   Car-like robots

Triggered by the impulse of car-likeness, boys – and often girls too – quickly construct vehicles. This phase of construction is mostly accompanied by (the boys') remarks such as: "Now we can add real 'formula one' decoration to it".

If no (car-like) models are given girls and boys often construct models with strong analogies to humans and animals. Merging abstract and concrete worlds, robotic materials are challenging. There is not just one right way to build a robot. Thus, many possibilities are found to tie to one's own imaginations and to follow one's own perceptions.

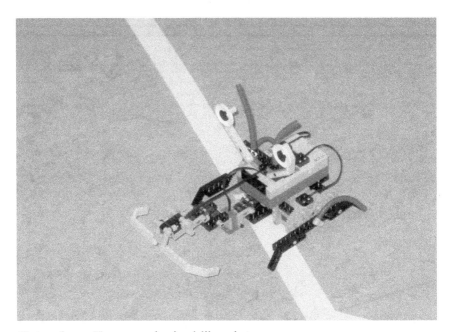

Picture 3:   Human- and animal-like robots

If the children are left to choose themselves their constructions are less gendered. Gender-specific behaviour becomes more obvious if given material, models and tasks already contain and enforce gender-specific orientations. Although the (Lego-) material evokes gender-specific behaviour[71], didactical interventions and gender-conscious tasks allow to deconstruct the gendered material. This point is

---

71   The offered combinations of wheels and engines often leads to the exclusion of other functional Lego bricks.

made very clear by robotics expert Deirdre Butler from St. Patrick's College, Dublin:

"(..) a teacher [...] noticed in her classroom [...] the fact that the boys' ideas were dominating and they all centered round wheels. They all had to be vehicles [...] that moved fast. So, what she said was - rather than separate the groups - [...] for your next project, [...] you cannot make a vehicle that moves on wheels. You can use wheels to make conveyor belts or to do anything else or create other moving parts [...] And she said, that was what began to change things in her classroom, because they began to make other types of things." (Interview with Deirdre Butler at the University of Bremen, 22.7.2004)

The task not to construct a wheeled vehicle can transform both internalised gender-specific behaviour and the use of gendered materials and should be combined with a gender sensitive view on team interaction and help.

Qualitative observation could not support the assumption that girls tend to work in a more team-oriented way than boys. In small groups, both sexes are able to develop social skills and prefer to work in groups. Though in some mixed teams, alternations between team work and a hierarchical division of tasks can be observed, these differences have more to do with the learning arrangement. This aspect became evident in themes such as moving the robot through a maze, where problem-solving strategies often got developed in teams. "Gender-neutral" themes helped to prevent mixed teams from falling apart into two separate gender groups.

When we anticipate gender differences we also discover that they can be actively transformed by both, the gendered material and the didactical design of the courses. The consequential "gender in the making" (Wiesner 2002) thereby takes place where material and didactical worlds interact in specific ways. Due to that, technical materiality and didactical intervention constitute a strong relation in Roberta courses, co-producing each other.

In that process, a gender-conscious didactical approach towards both, the technology and the students, becomes essential when it comes to presenting the robot to the group. Girls may be robbed of their fame: Often, the boys disturbed their presentations by letting their own robots drive into their's. The girls reacted to this in a gender stereotypic way: "You go ahead and start, we can present our robot at the end." Boys, on the other hand, were put under strong pressure by the amount of teacher attention. They failed in their "self-concept of the winner" (Buschmann 1994) in a row of unhappy presentations.

As we know today, bringing technology into schools can be beneficial but very much depends on the teachers. No wonder, the necessity of a gender sensitive training concept[72] for teachers is an important conclusion from the results of the qualitative evaluation. In Roberta courses, gender-sensitive teaching ensures that girls and boys have the same learning opportunities and thus amplifies the positive experience with technology design in medium and long term courses. Technological interest, creativity and the discovery of new skills and knowledge – perceived as a reflexive mingling of didactics and technology – can prepare children for an increasing interaction with technical objects, which will accompany and transform their lives. It is through this very concrete relation and interaction with both material and didactics, that, from our point of view, the specific potential of robotics in the promotion of technological interest for girls gets realised.

5   Conclusion

Our evaluation of robotics courses has shown the manifold potential these courses have for the technological empowerment of girls (and boys). As modern educational tools, robotics not only connect the life- and school-worlds of students but require an active stance towards technology. Through concrete handling, the robotics material supports the access to abstract concepts and, vice versa, the transfer of abstract concepts into concrete motions. The material itself provides feedback on how successful a construction or programming process is. If students experience technology as being shapeable in that way [73], they are not only given the possibility to handle digital media, but also to relate to these media in a creative and sustainable way. Used in a didactically careful fashion, robotics thus not only triggers and amplifies the interest of girls and women in technology but may even lead to the transformation of their orientations and strengthen their self-confidence. One of the most important reasons for that lies in the connection between constructing physical materials with software techniques, which offers a broad range of technologically oriented actions.

Our experiences with robotics to promote children's interests in technology allow conclusions that can be transferred to other educational concepts. Robotics is – for these reasons – an excellent medium for medial and technological education in schools. It is suitable as an interactive medium to generate boys' and girls' interest in technology. With that they might be more able to actively participate in a technologically mediated society. It is however also an appropriate medium for general education, in the more comprehensive sense of

---

72   Gender sensitive training concepts focus on the building of teams and learning communities, on the project themes offered, gender-sensitive interventions and on the gendered materials in use.
73   cf. Schelhowe 2001

the development of the personality and of access to a world that is more and more perceived and lived through technology. Robotics in schools require gender-sensitive didactics in order to ensure that the students have equal opportunities to develop and to design. Our insights can be summarized by the following didactical recommendations:

- Use designable technology
- Give opportunities for team work and promote team work
- Assist dynamic processes of team formation
- Promote open work and open learning scenarios
- Apply a flexible mix of open and structured learning
- Promote „gender-neutral" project themes
- Reflect help and guidance in a gender-conscious way
- Give performance-related feedback (particularly girls)
- Intervene in a gender-sensitive fashion during the project and presentation phases
- Deconstruct gendered material right from the beginning

Robotics technology – combined with a constructivist learning approach – then allows a less biased access. The use of robotics in classroom cannot solve all problems. If the life world of children gets integrated into the context of schools unquestioned, this can result in the transfer of the life world's gender constructions and their reproduction in day-to-day life at school.

References

AAUW (2000): Tech-Savvy: Educating Girls in the New Computer Age. American Association of University Women 2000.

Bühl, Achim; Zöfel, Peter (2004): SPSS 12. München: Pearson Studium.

Buschmann, Matthias (1994): Jungen und Koedukation. Zur Polarisierung der Geschlechterrollen. In: Die deutsche Schule 86 (11.2): 192-213.

Hartmann, Susann; Schecker, Horst (2005): Bietet Robotik Mädchen einen Zugang zu Informatik, Technik und Naturwissenschaft? Evaluationsergebnisse zu dem Projekt Roberta. In: Zeitschrift für Didaktik der Naturwissenschaften 11: 7-19.

Müllerburg, Monika; Petersen, Ulrike; Theidig, Gabriele (2004): Mit Robotern spielend lernen. In: VDI (eds.): Robotik 2004. VDI Berichte 2004 (1841): 393-400.

Papert, Seymour A. (1994): The Children's Machine: Rethinking School in the Age of Computer. New York: Basic Books

Schelhowe, Heidi (2001): Offene Technologie – Offene Kulturen. Zur Genderfrage im Projekt Virtuelle Internationale Frauenuniversität. In: FifF Kommunikation 2001 (3): 14-18.

Sjoberg, Svein (2002): Pupils' experiences and interests relating to science and technology – Some results from a comparative study in 21 countries. In: Stockholm Library of Curriculum Studies 2002 (available at http://folk.uio.no/sveinsj/ .

Turkle, Sherry (1984): The Second Self: Computers and the Human Spirit, New York: Simon and Schuster.

Wiesner, Heike (2002): Die Inszenierung der Geschlechter in den Naturwissenschaften. Wissenschafts- und Geschlechterforschung im Dialog. Frankfurt: Campus.

Wiesner, Heike (2004): Handlungsträgerschaft von Robotern: Robotik zur Förderung von Chancengleichheit im schulischen Bildungsbereich. In: Historical Social Research, Zentrum für Historische Sozialforschung 29 (4): 120-154.

About the Authors

Bath, Corinna

Corinna Bath, mathematician, is currently research fellow at the "Institute for Advanced Studies on Science, Technology and Society" in Graz, Austria. Recently, she finished the research project "Sociality with Machines" at the Department of Philosophy of Science at Vienna University, which focused on aspects of anthropomorphizing and gendering in current software agent research and robotics. Her dissertation project at the Computer Science Department at Bremen University, Germany, investigates theoretical foundations constituting the field of gender studies in computer science. She is particularly interested in the question of how to model "de-gendered" information technologies on the basis of existing computer science methods.
<bath@sts.tu-graz.at>

Björkman, Christina

Dr. Christina Björkman is a researcher in Technoscience Studies at Blekinge Institute of Technology, Sweden. Her main research focus concerns integration of feminist technoscience research into computer science. She has worked as a university lecturer in computer science since 1985.
<Christina.Bjorkman@bth.se>

Carstensen, Tanja

Tanja Carstensen, Sociologist, is research assistant in the working group "Work-Gender-Technology" at the Hamburg University of Technology, Germany. Her main work areas are Internet research, technology studies, technology in discourses, future of work, gender studies. www.tu-harburg.de/agentec
<carstensen@tu-harburg.de>

Crutzen, Cecile K.M.

Dr. Cecile K. M. Crutzen is an associate professor at the Open University of the Netherlands, School of Informatics, specialising in 'people, computers, and society'. She designs and develops course material and e-learning environments for distance education in computer science. Currently she is responsible for a "virtual design company" where students work in teams for the final part of their Bachelor's courses. She has prepared 'ambient intelligence' as a new topic for the Master in computer science. In her research, she investigates the relationship between computer science and gender studies with the aim of enriching computer science with a diversity of thinking and acting. http://cecile-crutzen.de/ <Cecile.Crutzen@ou.nl>

Elovaara, Pirjo

Dr. Pirjo Elovaara is senior lecturer in Technoscience Studies at the School of Technoculture, Humanities and Planning, Blekinge Institute of Technology, Sweden. Her main work area is feminist technoscience studies with the focus on design and use of information technology. She studies especially the concepts and practices of participation, agency, and relations and negotiations of human and non-human actors in the field of e-government including the domains of e-administration, e-services and e-democracy.
<Pirjo.Elovaara@bth.se>

Hanappi-Egger, Edeltraud

Dr. Edeltraud Hanappi-Egger holds a PhD in computer science and since 2002 she is professor for "Gender and Diversity in Organizations" at the Vienna University of Economics and Business Administration, Austria. Her main research areas are gender and software development, organization theory and organizational modelling with respect to gender issues and diversity management.
<Edeltraud.Hanappi-Egger@wu-wien.ac.at>

Hartmann, Susann

Dr. Susann Hartmann has been working on learning process studies and project evaluation at the University of Bremen, Germany. Her focus has been science education and student's conceptions in the field of mechanics. Gender-related studies were important in the two years she worked on the evaluation of robotics courses for girls. Currently she teaches at a local school.
<susann@uni-bremen.de>

Jensen, Heike

Dr. Heike Jensen is a postdoctoral researcher and lecturer at the Department of Gender Studies of Humboldt University in Berlin, Germany. Her research and teaching areas are media and media theories, women's movements and feminist media strategies, globalization and the Information Society. Her recent publications focus on the UN World Summit on the Information Society (WSIS), in which she actively participated: She was a member of the Steering Committee of the WSIS Gender Caucus and coordinated the European/North American Regional Conference on Gender and WSIS. She also was a civil society member of the German governmental delegation attending the Geneva and Tunis summit events.
<dr.heike.jensen@web.de>

Maass, Susanne

Dr. Susanne Maass is professor for „Gender and Informatics" in the Department for Mathematics/Computer Science and in the Center for Feminist Studies at Bremen University, Germany, since 1998. Her main work areas are socially-oriented software design, in particular from the gender perspective, requirements analysis, participatory software development, human-computer interaction, software-ergonomics in the context of service work, self-service concepts, e-commerce and customer orientation, the image and self image of informatics as a scientific discipline and a profession.
<maass@informatik.uni-bremen.de>

Meßmer, Ruth

Ruth Meßmer studied sociology and geography and works for the Forum of Competence "Gender Studies in Computer and Natural Sciences" [gin] in Freiburg, Germany, since 2002. She works on gender and diversity aspects in e-learning and is involved in the development of a blended learning tool for gender research in computer science and natural science. Here the conceptual design, the evaluation and the integration and adaption of innovative collaborative tools are her main work areas. Further interests and fields of activity are soft skills seminars for computer scientists and differences of team work in presence and in virtual teams. In 2006 she was external lecturer for "Gender and E-learning" at the University of Innsbruck, Austria.
<messmer@modell.iig.uni-freiburg.de>

Munk, Bettina
Bettina Munk is a visual artist based in Berlin, Germany. She took up a university teaching position for Programming in the Design Department at FHTW University of Applied Sciences Berlin in 2001. Since 2004, together with Yvonne Prätzel, she focuses on the design of girl-specific software.
<munk@logogo.org>

Paulitz, Tanja
Dr. Tanja Paulitz is a social and cultural scientist. She is assistant professor at the Centre for Interdisciplinary Studies on Women and Gender at the Technical University of Berlin, Germany. Since autumn 2006 on she is Lise-Meitner-Scholar at the Institute for Advanced Studies on Science, Technology and Society at Graz, Austria. Her main work areas are gender and ICTs, networks and virtual communities/subjectivities, feminist theories, methodologies and epistemologies in empirical research on science and technology, cultural studies of engineering knowledge. Her current research project is on "Gender and Engineering Design".
<tanja.paulitz@tu-berlin.de>

Rommes, Els
Dr. Els Rommes is assistant-professor for Gender, ICT and Pedagogy at the Institute for Gender Studies, Nijmegen University, Netherlands, and is coordinator of the Dutch PhD school Science, Technology and Modern Culture. Her research interests and main publication areas include strategies of inclusion of gender in the information society, gender sensitive design methodologies, participatory software development, women-only places on the Internet and women-only teaching, gendered images on gender and technology, domestication of computers and teenagers' gendered professional choices.
<E.Rommes@ped.kun.nl>

Schelhowe, Heidi
Dr. Heidi Schelhowe is professor for Digital Media in Education at the Department for Mathematics/Computer Science and member of the Center for Computing Technologies (TZI) at Bremen University, Germany. Her field of research and teaching is the application of digital media in schools as well as for university teaching and vocational training. She is head of an interdisciplinary team of about 15 researchers. Her special research interests are gender questions in computing science. She has been in charge of several research projects, e.g.

the Virtual International Women's University vifu; Gender and Information Society Technology GIST. www.dimeb.de
<schelhow@informatik.uni-bremen.de>

Schirmer, Carola

Carola Schirmer, sociologist, is research assistant in the working group „Gender and Informatics" in the Department for Mathematics/Computer Science and in the Center for Feminist Studies at Bremen University, Germany. Her research interests are in the fields of gender research in and on information technology and specifically the potential of participatory software development as part of gender-oriented design techniques. Her dissertation project focuses on the design of user interfaces for information retrieval as tools for improving users' information literacy.
<schirmer@informatik.uni-bremen.de>

Schmitz, Sigrid

Dr. Sigrid Schmitz has studied biology and is university lecturer on "Mediatization of the Natural Sciences and Gender Research" at the University of Freiburg, Germany, since 2002. Her main areas in teaching and research are gender aspects in the natural and computer sciences with particular focus on e-learning and user-oriented development of ICT applications, visualizations of digital body images, brain research, and the transdisciplinary dialogue between SET and the cultural-societal disciplines. Since 2002 she leads, together with Prof. Dr. Britta Schinzel, the Forum of Competence "Gender Studies in Computer and Natural Sciences" [gin]. She was Aigner-Rollett-visiting professor at the University of Graz, Austria, for Gender and Natural Sciences (2003), visiting lecturer at the University of Basel, Switzerland, (2004, 2006), and external lecturer for Gender and E-learning at the University of Innsbruck, Austria (2006).
<schmitz@modell.iig.uni-freiburg.de>

Trojer, Lena

Dr. Lena Trojer holds a professor chair in Information Technology and Gender Research at Faculty of Technology, Blekinge Institute of Technology, Sweden. She is heading the division Technoscience Studies at the same university. Her main research focus is on feminist technoscience in the context of information and communication technology.
<lena.trojer@bth.se>

Weber, Jutta
Dr. Jutta Weber is visiting professor at the Centre for Interdisciplinary Studies at the University of Duisburg-Essen as well as fellow of the research group 'Science in the Context of Application' (2006/07) at the Centre for Interdisciplinary Research (ZIF) at the University of Bielefeld. Her main research fields are technoscience studies, interdisciplinarity, philosophy of science, gender and media studies. Currently she is writing a book on "Travelling Models, Metaphors and Machines: The Politics of Translation in Technoscience and Its Studies".
<jutta.weber@uni-due.de>

Winker, Gabriele
Dr. Gabriele Winker is professor for occupational science and gender studies at the Hamburg University of Technology, heading the working group "Work-Gender-Technology". Her research priorities are Internet research, technoscience, flexible work patterns – particularly from gender perspectives. www.tu-harburg.de/agentec
<winker@tu-harburg.de>

Wiesner, Heike
Dr. Heike Wiesner is visiting professor at the Berlin School of Economics in the Harriet Taylor-Mill-Institute with the denomination "Knowledge Management, eLearning and Gender", Germany. Her main work areas are business informatics and eLearning, science and technology studies, gender and digital media. She is the author of the book „Die Inszenierung der Geschlechter in den Naturwissenschaften", Campus.
<wiesner@heike-wiesner.de>

Wiesner-Steiner, Andreas
Dr. Andreas Wiesner-Steiner has conducted research at the Research Centre Sustainability and the working group Digital Media in Education, both at the University Bremen, Germany. His main work areas are science and technology studies and sociology of technology (digital media, robotics in education, climate change, human genome research).
<awiesner@informatik.uni-bremen.de>

Zorn, Isabel
Isabel Zorn is research assistant at the centre for Digital Media and Education at the Department for Mathematics/Computer Science of Bremen University, Ger-

many. She was responsible for the scientific management of the International Symposium on Gender and Information Society GIST 2004.Her main research interests are the interlinkage of technology design and education, gender awareness in technology construction, international virtual communities and social software and educational aspects of robot construction.
<izorn@informatik.uni-bremen.de>

Geschlechterforschung

Ruth Becker / Beate Kortendiek (Hrsg.)
**Handbuch Frauen-
und Geschlechterforschung**
Theorie, Methoden, Empirie
2004. 736 S.
Br. EUR 34,90
ISBN 3-8100-3926-8

Geb. EUR 49,90
ISBN 3-531-14278-X

Robert W. Connell
Der gemachte Mann
Konstruktion und Krise
von Männlichkeiten
3. Aufl. 2006. 304 S. Br. EUR 24,90
ISBN 3-531-14627-0

Sabine Grenz
(Un)heimliche Lust
Über den Konsum sexueller
Dienstleistungen
2005. 255 S. Br. EUR 29,90
ISBN 3-531-14776-5

Arlie Hochschild
Keine Zeit
Wenn die Firma zum Zuhause wird
und zu Hause nur Arbeit wartet
2. Aufl. 2006. XXXVIII, 305 S.
Br. EUR 19,90
ISBN 3-531-14468-5

Martina Löw / Bettina Mathes (Hrsg.)
**Schlüsselwerke
der Geschlechterforschung**
2005. 324 S. Geb. EUR 34,90
ISBN 3-531-13886-3

Sigrid Metz-Göckel
**Exzellenz und Elite im amerika-
nischen Hochschulsystem**
Portrait eines Women's College
2004. 310 S. Br. EUR 26,90
ISBN 3-8100-3711-7

Irene Villa
Sexy Bodies
Eine soziologische Reise
durch den Geschlechtskörper
3., überarb. Aufl. 2006. 319 S.
Br. EUR 24,90
ISBN 3-531-14481-2

Ulrike Vogel (Hrsg.)
**Wege in die Soziologie
und die Frauen- und
Geschlechterforschung**
Autobiographische Notizen
der ersten Generation von
Professorinnen an der Universität
2006. 320 S. Geb. EUR 24,90
ISBN 3-531-14966-0

Christine Weinbach
Systemtheorie und Gender
Das Geschlecht im Netz der Systeme
2004. 206 S. Br. EUR 25,90
ISBN 3-531-14178-3

Erhältlich im Buchhandel oder beim Verlag.
Änderungen vorbehalten. Stand: Juli 2006.

www.vs-verlag.de

VS VERLAG FÜR SOZIALWISSENSCHAFTEN

Abraham-Lincoln-Straße 46
65189 Wiesbaden
Tel. 0611.7878-722
Fax 0611.7878-400